WEALTH

How to Get It
How to Keep It

WEALTH

How to Get It
How to Keep It

*The H.D. Vest System
for Achieving Financial Security*

*Herb D. Vest, CFP, CPA, CLU
Lynn R. Niedermeier, CPA, CFS*

amacom
American Management Association

New York · Atlanta · Boston · Chicago · Kansas City · San Francisco · Washington, D.C.
Brussels · Tokyo · Toronto · Mexico City

This book is available at a special
discount when ordered in bulk quantities.
For information, contact Special Sales Department,
AMACOM, a division of American Management Association,
135 West 50th Street, New York, NY 10020.

Library of Congress Cataloging-in-Publication Data

Vest, Herb D.
    Wealth, how to get it, how to keep it : the H. D. Vest system for achieving financial security / Herb D. Vest, Lynn Niedermeier.
        p.   cm.
    Includes index.
    ISBN 0–8144–0212–7
    1. Finance, Personal.   2. Wealth.   I. Niedermeier, Lynn.
II. Title.
HG179.V47   1993
332.024—dc20   93–27106
                                                                    CIP

Printing number

10 9 8 7 6 5 4 3 2

Table of Contents

4 Sources of Income—A Road Map to Investment Options: Line 7   **58**

5 A Snapshot of Your Personal Finances— Interest, Dividends, Diversification, and Annuities: Lines 8a, 8b, and 9   **71**

6 From Self-Employment to Social Security— Making Tax-Wise Investments: Lines 12–19, 21, 26, and 27   **87**

7 Using Your Individual Retirement Account to Create Wealth: Line 24   **97**

Preface

A great pleasure in life is doing what people say you cannot do.

Walter Bagehot

The dream of attaining wealth, and the financial freedom that goes with it, is nearly universal. Virtually everyone wants enough money for an attractive home, quality college education for their children, a comfortable lifestyle, and a secure and enriching retirement.

But though all these goals are widely pursued, few know how to achieve them. For the vast majority, the idea of accumulating wealth and attaining financial freedom seems like an impossible dream. Pie-in-the-sky.

That's unfortunate, because it does not have to be that way. The fact is, almost everyone can accumulate wealth and achieve a level of financial security. What it takes is discipline and a knowledge of how to manage your money for long-term goals rather than solely for immediate gratification and consumerism. This money management process need not be complex. You don't have to be a financial expert to make it work.

That's where *Wealth: How to Get It, How to Keep It* comes into play. This book guides you through the financial planning process using a unique tool—your federal tax return Form 1040. With the proper use of this document, which we will outline step-by-step in this book, you can analyze your financial situation and develop strategies for achieving your financial goals. And, unlike most financial planning guides, because this is based on your tax return, you will be developing a plan custom-tailored to your financial status.

Wealth: How to Get It, How to Keep It will help you to do the following:

* Make annual assessments of your financial situation.
* Educate yourself about the financial planning process.
* Discipline yourself to save and invest for the future.

* Structure your current investments to support your personal goals and attain financial freedom.
* Identify the best ways to provide for your children's education.
* Analyze your insurance needs to determine if you are properly protected.
* Identify strategies for reducing and deferring your tax liability.
* Develop a plan to provide for a financially secure retirement.

In creating your blueprint for financial freedom, we will focus on these broad areas of financial planning—insurance, education, taxes, retirement, and estates—as well as on achieving the goal of overall financial security. Although it is vitally important to build a nest egg to allow for a comfortable and dignified retirement, it is equally important to provide for security during the working years. All too many people, even those with substantial incomes, are simply a paycheck away from the poverty line. With little or no savings and investments, they have nothing to fall back on should they lose their jobs or suffer an extraordinary expense. Our blueprint for financial freedom will provide techniques and strategies for building a rainy day fund that can appreciate rapidly.

In each major area we review the relevant issues as well as recommended solutions and strategies. For example, you will learn how to trade up from low-yielding certificates of deposit and money market funds to low-risk investments that can build substantial value over the years.

Related to this, you will come to understand the power of compounding and diversification and how you can harness these powers in your investment portfolio, even if you invest only modest sums of money. Did you know that investing just $200 per month could yield more than $450,000 in 30 years? And that an investment of $500 per month could produce over $1 million? It's true—and we will provide you with a road map for producing similar results with your investments.

The idea is to provide you with the know-how to employ the various tools of financial planning at your disposal. Armed with this knowledge, you can control your destiny, achieving the kind of lifestyle and security you may have thought were well beyond your means.

This book is based on real-world experience. As tax and financial professionals, we and our colleagues have helped thousands of people use their tax returns as a blueprint for developing personalized plans designed to achieve financial freedom. If you are wondering how a tax return can serve as a financial guide, there is really no mystery. That's because the tax return provides a revealing snapshot of how you spend your money, how much money you are saving, the kinds of investments you are making, and the assets you have and need to protect. This information is the starting point for devising an intelligent and effective wealth-building program.

Wealth: How to Get It, How to Keep It assists you in analyzing your tax return by identifying key areas you should review and providing strategies for correcting weaknesses, bolstering strong points, and integrating all of your finances into a master plan.

Acknowledgments

We cannot overstate our gratitude to the employees and representatives of H. D. Vest Financial Services, who today number more than 4,000 nationwide. These individuals have been instrumental in the implementation of our approach to personal finance and investment planning; they have also greatly enriched our lives and those of our clients.

We would like to thank our families, without whose support this book could never have been written. Barbara Vest, Daniel and Matthew, Mike Vlies, Erica and Beau: Your patience, love, and encouragement will never be forgotten.

Thanks also to Steve Hastings and Patricia Bellows, who—with dedication and brilliance—have helped guide H. D. Vest since its early years.

In preparing this book, we relied heavily on the knowledge and insight of Mike Perkins, CFP, CFS; Scott Tatum, CFP, CFS; Carol J. Henry, CFP, CLU; Jeff Klein, CFS; Robin Campbell, CFP, CIMA; Maurice D. Olson, CFP; Hilary Wells, CFP, CFS; Susan Saulter, CFS; and Candace Talmadge, all of whom work with us at H. D. Vest's central office in Irving, Texas.

We appreciate the efforts of Scott Baradell, who edited the text, and the rest of our Corporate Communications Department: Barbara Turner, Vaughn Anthony, Tammy Noles, and Lolly Briano. Thanks also go to Andrea Pedolsky of AMACOM Books, whose thoughtful suggestions improved the manuscript.

Finally, we thank the thousands of American families and small businesses that have discovered the wisdom of investment planning through H. D. Vest's network of tax and financial professionals. If you are not currently among them, we hope that through this book, you soon will be.

How to Use This Book

Think of this book as an interactive guide that takes you, line by line, from your tax return to our proven strategies for attaining financial freedom. With this in mind, take your most recent tax return out of your filing cabinet and, as you proceed through this book, fill out the Taxpayer Profile in Appendix A. The Taxpayer Profile provides a "To Do" list of priorities for putting your financial affairs in order and, in turn, for getting on the road to financial freedom. When it is time for you to refer to the Profile, the following symbol will appear: ✳

Here's how it works: Refer, for example, to Lines 8a and 9 of Form 1040; the lines concern taxable interest and dividends. When reviewing these lines in Chapter 5, you will turn to section C of the Taxpayer Profile, which asks about your current investments and income level, and—on the basis of your answers—offers a to-do list of recommendations for improving your financial position. As you consider the options and strategies presented in Chapter 5, you will be able to respond to suggestions that you transfer assets from CDs to higher-yielding assets, consider tax-advantaged investments such as annuities, or follow other recommendations that apply to your specific situation.

The Profile should encourage you to develop a list of questions, ideas, and concerns regarding your finances—an excellent starting point for consultation with a tax and financial professional who can help you move ahead in developing your personal financial plan.

Now let's talk money.

WEALTH

How to Get It
How to Keep It

Chapter 1

The 1040: Your Blueprint for Financial Freedom

Put not your trust in money, but put your money in trust.
Oliver Wendell Holmes

When Benjamin Franklin noted that "it's not how much you make that counts, but how much you keep," he was stating a simple but often overlooked rule of money management.

Consider this: If, like most people, you think that "money management" means keeping tabs on how much you are earning, looking forward to your next raise or bonus, and keeping a lid on personal spending to keep from going overboard on credit card charges, you see money as simply a means of paying for goods and services. Cash comes in and cash goes out. Financial success, from this all too common perspective, is just a matter of raising the volume of cash (through raises or bonuses) that flows in and out of your checking account.

But this approach to "money management" ignores the wisdom of old Ben's axiom. Take the case of three families earning $50,000, $100,000, and $1 million a year, respectively. If each family spends the sum total of its earnings, all three are equivalent from one key standpoint: They are doing little or nothing to create wealth.

Much like the $50,000-a-year family, the $1-million-a-year clan may be just a paycheck away from financial disaster. Without savings and investments, families and individuals are hostages to economic setbacks (such as the loss of a job) and are unable to put capital to work for such long-term goals as children's college education and a comfortable retirement. For this reason, the $50,000-a-year family that invests $200 a month may be more financially secure and ultimately wealthier than the $1-million-a-year family that spends all of its earnings.

So why do so many Americans fail to invest any part of their income? Often, nonsavers insist that, after housing, food, medical, clothing, and education bills, there isn't enough left to start a wealth-building program.

1

Pay Yourself First

In most cases, this argument is unfounded. In seeking to counter the myth that expenses take every last dollar of discretionary income, two factors must be considered:

1. *Virtually everyone with a steady income can set aside some portion of that income to invest; all it takes is discipline.* Think of investment discipline as "paying yourself first." We are all bombarded by advertisements for cars, televisions, vacations, clothing. In this environment, the temptation to buy first and save last (if there is anything left to save) is great, but it reverses the correct order of financial priorities. By paying yourself (thus making an investment in your future) before you pay for a car, a sweater, or a dinner on the town, you are building a foundation for wealth creation and financial security.

If you lack the discipline to stop spending and start investing, consider participating in a mutual fund or other periodic investment program that automatically withdraws a monthly sum from your checking account. This imposes discipline because money out of your grasp is money you cannot spend. In time, you will gain great satisfaction—and peace of mind—from seeing your automatic investments accumulate in a wealth-building portfolio.

2. *You can launch a successful wealth-building program with modest monthly investments.* If you have been holding back because you are convinced that it "doesn't pay" to put aside as little as $100 or even $50 a month, it's time to reevaluate your thinking. With the power of compounding working for you, even a small percentage of your paycheck each week or month can make you rich over time.

For example, investing $100 per month at 10% (compounded annu-

Exhibit 1-1. How small investments can add up to big savings.

Monthly Investment	5 Years	10 Years	15 Years	20 Years	25 Years	30 Years	35 Years
$ 25	1,936	5,121	10,362	18,984	33,171	56,512	94,916
$ 50	3,871	10,242	20,723	37,968	66,342	113,024	189,832
$100	7,743	20,484	41,447	75,937	132,683	226,049	379,664
$200	15,487	40,969	82,894	151,874	265,367	452,097	759,327
$500	38,718	102,422	207,235	379,684	663,416	1,130,244	1,898,319

Assumes a 10% rate of return, compounded monthly, with interest and dividends reinvested.

ally with interest and dividends reinvested) gives you $7,743 in 5 years, $20,484 in 10 years, $75,937 in 20 years, and more than $200,000 ($226,049 to be exact) in 30 years. Boosting the monthly investment to $200 yields $15,487 in 5 years, $40,969 in 10 years, $151,874 in 20 years, and $452,097 in 30 years. And when we step up to $500 a month—a very affordable figure for many families and individuals—the payoff is $379,684 in 20 years, over $1 million in 30 years, and nearly $2 million ($1,898,319) in 35 years.

These facts are illustrated in Exhibits 1-1 and 1-2.

Why You Should Start Today

With the awesome power of compounding, the longer money is invested, the more it will produce for you (see Exhibit 1-3). Thus, the reason to begin a systematic investment program now. For example, if you begin

Exhibit 1-2. How values build when you make regular investments of $100 a month.

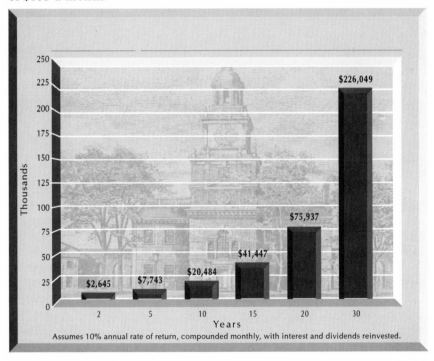

Assumes 10% annual rate of return, compounded monthly, with interest and dividends reinvested.

Exhibit 1-3. How the earlier you start investing for retirement, the more you have.

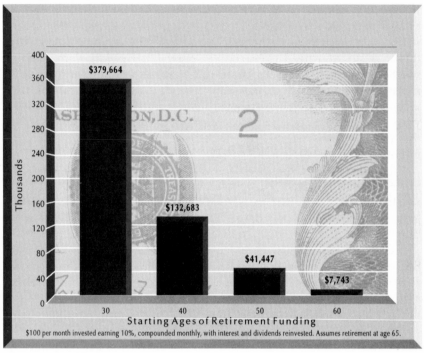

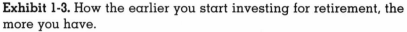

$100 per month invested earning 10%, compounded monthly, with interest and dividends reinvested. Assumes retirement at age 65.

investing $100 a month at age 30, you will have $379,664 by the retirement age of 65 (again, assuming, a 10% compounded annual return). If you wait until age 40 the nest egg drops to $132,683. And if you don't begin until age 50, the total is only $41,447, falling all the way to $7,743 if you begin investing at age 60.

Certainly, it is never too late to start investing. Even a modest nest egg is better than none at all. But the key point is that the earlier you start to invest, the longer and harder your money can work for you, producing a larger sum for the purchase of a home, a college education, an investment in a business, or a source of retirement income.

When the returns from systematic investing are so substantial, why do so many people—perhaps you, too—do nothing to build wealth?

A major reason is psychological: People cannot picture themselves suffering a serious financial reversal. They cannot imagine that someday they might find themselves without a job to go to (and, in turn, without a paycheck to bring home). The only way to prepare for this, or for another major setback, is to achieve some measure of financial independence.

Even if you are never dismissed or laid off from your job, at some point in your life you will want to retire comfortably, to enjoy that special period as a reward for all the years of hard work that came before. With this in mind, you need to transport yourself to the future and draw a mental picture of where you want to be and how you want to live. To make this vision a reality, pause now and ask yourself a critical question: How much money do I need to achieve my financial goals and how many years do I have to accumulate the necessary funds? Only by answering this question can you determine (referring to Exhibit 1-3) how much money you must start investing now.

This goal-setting process is a key to successful money management. Simply saying "I want to make a lot of money and get filthy rich" is a daydream, not a goal. Only about 5% of Americans set specific financial goals, and, in turn, only 5% of us retire with financial dignity. The correlation between goal setting and financial independence is unmistakable.

Consider that retirement income can come from three major sources: Social Security, a company-sponsored pension or profit-sharing plan, and personal savings. Perhaps you have been saving modestly to this point, assuming that the first two components of your retirement nest egg will provide the lion's share of the income.

If so, you may be falling into a dangerous trap that will leave you far short of the income needed for a comfortable retirement. Here's why: First, if you are under age 50, there is reason to doubt that Social Security will be in force when you need it. And even if it is, the benefit it provides will undoubtedly be less than you need.

Looking on the bright side, let's assume that your employer maintains a pension or profit-sharing plan that provides income at retirement. In most cases, these plans replace 30–40% of your income. Although your financial needs may decline at retirement, chances are they will not decline significantly—certainly not by 60–70%. With this in mind, you will have to find some way to close the gap between what your plan (and possible Social Security) pays and what you need to live well. That's where an intelligent plan for saving and investing comes into play, and that's why it is so critical. Perhaps your parents, and their parents, could rely on "the company" and "the government" to provide for them. Chances are you will have to be far more self-reliant.

So when we talk about successful money management, we are really talking about planning. The two are inextricably related. Do you want to retire? At some point in your life, you will likely want to or have to stop working. Finances must be in place to provide for that day. And there are many other issues, variables, goals, and contingencies that financial planning must address:

* Do you want to send your children to college?
* Do you recognize the need to protect yourself against various risks?
* Are you in debt?
* Do you want to get out from under the terrible pressure of mounting bills?
* Do you save any money? If so, do you put it all in the bank?
* Is there a better place to invest your money?
* Which investments are most appropriate for you given your age, income, and goals?

Financial management encompasses all of these issues. It is a matter of establishing goals and setting out to achieve them. Whatever your goals, the idea is to think about them, to write them down, to start visualizing the future and how you want it to look for you in 5 years, 10 years, 20 years, 50 years. From this exercise you can begin to calculate just how much money you will need to achieve your goals.

The Investment Dilemma: Return, Inflation, and Taxes

For many of you, the discipline to save and invest for the future may be no problem at all. In fact, you may have modest or substantial sums of money invested in a limited or broad range of investments. And yet, in all likelihood, you remain uncertain as to whether these investments are right for your age, means, tax bracket, and goals.

Like so many people, you have good intentions but little understanding of money and investing. What investment options are available to you? What is the best way to choose from among them? You're just not sure.

Hence, when it comes to finances, most people simply react. They may hear of an investment vehicle, perhaps a real estate limited partnership or a municipal bond fund, and invest in that vehicle without seriously considering its merits (or lack of them) and where it fits in their total financial picture. What we are saying to them is "Stop! Take a closer look at this thing called money and start building a master plan for how to manage it. Factor in your goals, your taxes, your insurance, your upside potential, and your downside risk." The idea is to take a holistic approach toward your finances.

All too many people believe that there are only two categories of investments: "good" and "bad." Good investments are those perceived to be guaranteed (such as Treasury bills and bank certificates of deposit); bad investments are deemed to carry an element of risk. The problem with this simplistic view of personal finance is that it fails to consider that there is some risk involved in *every* investment, and, equally important, there is a risk involved in *not* investing and in failing to take prudent risk.

For example, you may believe the widely held assumption that a bank CD yielding a 5% rate of interest is a sound investment. "It is relatively risk-free," you say, "with a respectable return." At first blush, you appear to be correct. But two key factors—the impact of taxes and of inflation—have been overlooked.

EXAMPLE: Hernandez invests $10,000 in a 5% CD. He earns an annual interest income of $500. That may look fine, but wait. Assuming Hernandez is in the 31% (combined state and federal) tax bracket, we have to subtract $155, leaving a balance of $345. Then, factoring in a modest 3.1% inflation rate (as of 1992) on the $10,000, we must subtract another $310. The effects of this double whammy are shocking: Hernandez finds that his return after taxes and inflation is not $500 but $35, producing a real return of less than 1% (0.35% to be exact).

What looked on the surface to be a safe investment (and thus, based on our prior thinking, a "good" investment) turned out to be a disaster. Not the kind of traumatic disaster we see when an uninsured investment collapses, but a disaster nevertheless. That's because when your real return is reduced by inflation, your money slowly but inevitably loses its buying power and thus shrivels up. As Exhibit 1-4 indicates, after the double whammy, even a 12% rate of return winds up losing value.

Exhibits 1-5 and 1-6 reveal how quickly money erodes and loses its power—from the ravages of inflation alone.

Now let's engage in a little self-assessment. How are your "good" investments faring? More to the point, are they as good as you think they are? To calculate what you are really earning, complete this worksheet for each of your investments.

1. Original investment amount $_____
2. Earnings rate   _____%
3. Investment income
   (#1 × #2)   _____
4. Inflation rate   _____%

Exhibit 1-4. The effect of inflation and taxes on investment yields.

	INTEREST RATE								
	4%	5%	6%	7%	8%	9%	10%	11%	12%
Annual Interest Income	400	500	600	700	800	900	1000	1100	1200
Taxes (28%)	−112	−140	−168	−196	−224	−252	−280	−308	−336
Return After Tax	288	360	432	504	576	648	720	792	864
Inflation (3.1%)*	−310	−310	−310	−310	−310	−310	−310	−310	−310
Return After Inflation	−22	50	122	194	266	338	410	482	554
Real Rate of Return	−0.22%	0.50%	1.22%	1.94%	2.66%	3.38%	4.10%	4.82%	5.54%

*Inflation rate based on percentage increase in Consumer Price Index for Urban Consumers from December 1991 to December 1992.

Exhibit 1-5. How inflation reduces the value of $10,000.

Inflation Rate	5 Years	10 Years	15 Years	20 Years
4%	8,219	6,756	5,553	4,564
5%	7,835	6,139	4,810	3,769
6%	7,473	5,584	4,173	3,118

Exhibit 1-6. Amount required to maintain purchasing power of $10,000.

Inflation Rate	5 Years	10 Years	15 Years	20 Years
4%	12,167	14,802	18,009	21,911
5%	12,763	16,289	20,789	26,533
6%	13,382	17,908	23,966	32,071

5. Inflation loss
   (#1 × #4)   _____

6. Taxes (#3 × current tax
   bracket)
   (if taxable)   _____

7. Return after inflation and taxes
   (#3 −{#5 + #6})   _____

8. Rate of return adjusted for
   taxes and inflation (#7/#1)   _____ %

Surprised? Disappointed? You're not alone. Time and again, a little mathematics proves that "good" investments do not ensure financial independence. Still, the "safety alone" trap is an easy one to fall into. To illustrate this, let's look at the case of two fictitious couples, the Bennetts and the Sorensens (see Exhibit 1-7).

In 1976, each couple invested $200,000, both as a nest egg for retirement and to provide an income stream to help with current expenses.

THE BENNETTS: The Bennetts put their money into a fixed-income investment that offered them 9.54%. As a result, they received $19,080 in interest on their $200,000. The Bennetts thought they were safe. "With an investment that pays 9.54% a year," they concluded, "we have no worries about inflation. We're set for life."

Exhibit 1-7. How income from $200,000 invested in a 9.54% fixed income account compares with income from $200,000 invested in an equity growth fund.

$200,000 Invested in a Hypothetical 9.54% Fixed Income Account

Original Investment $200,000

Total Interest Received
from 1976 to 1990. . . . . . . $286,200

Value of Investment
on December 31, 1990. . . . $200,000

Annual interest income is based on initial investment.

Illustration shows the first year, fifth year and each five-year interval thereafter.

Income From $200,000 Invested in an Equity Growth Fund

Original Investment $200,000

Total Amount Withdrawn
from 1976 to 1990. . . . . . . $329,258

Value of Investment
on December 31, 1990. . . . $411,397

9.54% annual withdrawals, beginning December 1, 1976 and every twelve months thereafter, are based on the account balance and not on the initial investment.

Illustration shows the first year, fifth year and each five-year interval thereafter.

Results include the effects of the applicable sales charge, which for an investment of $200,000 would have been 3.5%.

Income From $200,000 Invested in a 9.54% Fixed Income Account

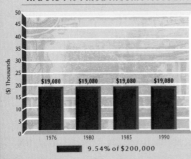

9.54% of $200,000

Income From $200,000 Invested in an Equity Growth Fund

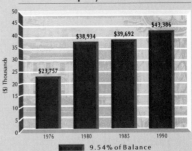

9.54% of Balance

The graphs compare how the Bennetts and the Sorensens fared. At the end of 1976, the Sorensens withdrew $23,757 from their equity growth fund an amount close to the $19,080 earned by the Bennetts. The real difference in the two investments became apparent as time went by. By 1980, the Sorensens' annual 9.54% withdrawal had grown to 38,934. Ten years later, in 1990, it had increased to $43,386. But in 1990 the Bennetts were still receiving $19,080.

The Bennetts still had their original nest egg of $200,000 at the end of 1990. They found some comfort in that fact. But the Sorensens were even more comfortable with the growth of their nest egg in an equity growth fund—it had more than doubled over the years, to $411,397!

By now you should know that they based their financial security on a false assumption. Consider what has happened to the purchasing power of the Bennetts' money. In 1976, it was quite possible for a couple to retire on $19,080 a year. That's certainly not true today, because the cost of living has increased by more than 140%. In other words, it takes $2.41 to buy what $1.00 bought in 1976. Of course, the Bennetts still have their $200,000 nest egg, but that too will buy less than half of what it used to.

The Bennetts did not understand how savagely inflation would eat away at the purchasing power of their dollars. Their "safe" investment turned out to be not so safe after all.

THE SORENSENS: The Sorensens, on the other hand, understood that the only "safe" investment was one that would protect their purchasing power. They realized that they would need more and more income in the years ahead and that their original investment would also need to grow.

With this in mind, the Sorensens decided to invest in an equity growth mutual fund, reinvesting all of their dividends and capital gain distributions. They also decided to make withdrawals of 9.54% percent each year based on the value of their account at the end of the previous year.

The Sorensens recognized that the value of their investment and the amount of their withdrawals each year were not guaranteed and would fluctuate. But they felt that their mutual fund's investment objective of long-term capital growth plus income was right for them.

The Sorensens' first withdrawal was $23,757. By 1980, the Sorensens were able to take out $38,934. By 1985, their annual withdrawal was $39,692. And by 1990, it had grown to $43,386. At the same time, the Bennetts (with their "safe" investment) were still getting checks for a relatively meager $19,080 a year.

The Sorensens have another enormous advantage over the Bennetts. At the end of 1990, the Bennetts' investment was still worth $200,000 but the value of the Sorensens' investment had grown to more than $411,000. Imagine how much peace of mind that brought the Sorensens (as well as affording them the flexibility to enjoy the extra luxuries of life).

* * * *

Let's stop briefly to sum up what we have learned to this point:

1. The risks involved in simply putting your money in "safekeeping"—whether in a CD or, worse yet, under your mattress—are very real. The double whammy of inflation and taxation are poised to steal your

money away from you, specifically in terms of what that money can purchase, which is the only real value money has.

2. The inability to visualize long-term needs and objectives, and how to achieve them, is a major reason people fail to reach financial independence. Lack of discipline is another critical factor that dooms most people to financial insecurity.

3. Fortunately, there is a proven way to create wealth, and, in turn, to build a solid foundation for a secure and prosperous life. As we have noted, it is little more than sound financial planning.

This is the process by which you set your goals, map out a course of action to reach those goals, and then begin making the necessary investments to put your plan in motion. This process requires that you discard all your simplistic notions about "good" and "bad" investments, that you clean out the cobwebs in your mind and open yourself to learning new concepts. Equally important, the process requires the discipline to make a commitment to your future.

How Much Will It Take?

The dollar value of your commitment depends on the level of your earnings, the nature of your goals, and the time you have to achieve those goals. All too often, people are told to base their financial management on arbitrary numbers. For example, you will often hear the "guideline" that you should set aside 10–20% of your income for savings or investment. Those are nice round figures, but they may be woefully inadequate.

Rather than base your monthly or annual investments on an arbitrary figure, ask yourself what you want to achieve and when you want to achieve it. Assume, for example, that you and your spouse are earning a combined income of $80,000. If your goal is to ensure a comfortable retirement, you will need at least 75% of your current income ($60,000 a year) at retirement.

The best way to provide that is to build an investment portfolio capable of producing sufficient income ($60,000 adjusted upward for inflation) for your retirement. How much it will take to do that depends on how long you have to invest. If you are 25 years old and just beginning your career (which is the best time to lay the groundwork for long-term goals), investing 10% of your steadily growing income may be sufficient to meet your financial objectives. But if you are 50 years old and just getting started in wealth building, you must substantially accelerate the investment process, salting away 30% or more of your income for the next 15 to 20 years.

Our point is that you should ignore the oft-cited arbitrary guidelines associated with financial planning in favor of those that pertain to your specific means and objectives. This is the only way to achieve your financial goals.

To accurately calculate your needs for financial independence, work through the following exercise:

What Do You Need to Achieve Financial Independence?

1. Calculate the estimated annual income you will need at retirement by matching up your age and current annual income in the chart below. Round both numbers to the next higher range.   _____

	Current Annual Income ($)										
Age	30,000	40,000	50,000	60,000	70,000	80,000	100,000	125,000	150,000	175,000	200,000
35	129,229	172,305	215,381	258,457	301,533	344,609	430,762	538,452	646,143	753,833	861,524
40	96,567	128,756	160,945	193,134	225,323	257,512	321,890	402,363	482,835	563,308	643,781
45	72,161	96,214	120,268	144,321	168,375	192,428	240,535	300,669	360,803	420,936	481,070
50	53,923	71,897	89,871	107,845	125,819	143,793	179,742	224,677	269,613	314,548	359,484
55	40,294	53,725	67,157	80,588	94,019	107,451	134,314	167,892	201,470	235,049	268,627
60	30,110	40,147	50,183	60,220	70,257	80,294	100,367	125,459	150,550	200,734	200,734

Note: Estimated annual retirement income assumes 75% of current income needed to maintain present standard of living at retirement; average salary increases of 6%; and retirement at age 65.

2. Calculate the estimated annual Social Security benefits you are likely to receive at retirement by matching up your age and current annual income in the chart below. Round both numbers to the next higher range.   _____

	Current Annual Income ($)										
Age	**30,000**	**40,000**	**50,000**	**60,000**	**70,000**	**80,000**	**100,000**	**125,000**	**150,000**	**175,000**	**200,000**
	Single/With Working Spouse										
35	13,980 / 20,964	15,876 / 23,808	16,836 / 25,248	16,836 / 25,248	16,836 / 25,248	16,836 / 25,248	16,836 / 25,248	16,836 / 25,248	16,836 / 25,248	16,836 / 25,248	16,836 / 25,248
40	13,398 / 20,094	15,132 / 22,692	15,960 / 23,934	15,960 / 23,934	15,960 / 23,934	15,960 / 23,934	15,960 / 23,934	15,960 / 23,934	15,960 / 23,934	15,960 / 23,934	15,960 / 23,934
45	12,816 / 19,224	14,388 / 21,576	15,084 / 22,620	15,084 / 22,620	15,084 / 22,620	15,084 / 22,620	15,084 / 22,620	15,084 / 22,620	15,084 / 22,620	15,084 / 22,620	15,084 / 22,620
50	12,126 / 18,186	13,374 / 20,058	13,920 / 20,874	13,920 / 20,874	13,920 / 20,874	13,920 / 20,874	13,920 / 20,874	13,920 / 20,874	13,920 / 20,874	13,920 / 20,874	13,920 / 20,874
55	11,436 / 17,148	12,360 / 18,540	12,756 / 19,128	12,756 / 19,128	12,756 / 19,128	12,756 / 19,128	12,756 / 19,128	12,756 / 19,128	12,756 / 19,128	12,756 / 19,128	12,756 / 19,128
60	10,764 / 16,140	11,484 / 17,226	11,772 / 17,652	11,772 / 17,652	11,772 / 17,652	11,772 / 17,652	11,772 / 17,652	11,772 / 17,652	11,772 / 17,652	11,772 / 17,652	11,772 / 17,652

Note: Social Security projections assume retirement at age 65 with maximum contributions made. Estimates based on Social Security Administration data.

3. Calculate the estimated annual company pension benefits you are likely to receive at retirement by matching up your age and current annual income in the chart below. Round both numbers to the next higher range. _____

	Current Annual Income ($)										
Age	**30,000**	**40,000**	**50,000**	**60,000**	**70,000**	**80,000**	**100,000**	**125,000**	**150,000**	**175,000**	**200,000**
35	45,230	60,307	75,383	90,460	105,537	120,613	150,767	188,458	226,150	268,842	301,533
40	33,798	45,065	56,331	67,597	78,863	90,129	112,662	140,827	168,992	197,158	225,323
45	25,256	33,675	42,094	50,512	58,931	67,350	84,187	105,234	126,281	147,328	168,375
50	18,873	25,164	31,455	37,746	44,037	50,328	62,910	78,637	94,364	110,092	125,819
55	14,103	18,804	23,505	28,206	32,907	37,608	47,010	58,762	70,515	82,267	94,019
60	10,538	14,051	17,564	21,077	24,590	28,103	35,128	43,911	52,693	61,475	70,257

Note: Assumes average pension benefit at a payout of 35% of income needed at retirement; average salary increases of 6%; retirement at age 65. If you do not have access to a company pension plan, place a zero in the appropriate space.

4. Calculate the estimated investment income you are likely to receive annually at retirement by matching up your age and current value of savings and investments. Exclude primary residence and

personal property. Round age and current value of
savings and investments to the next higher range. _____

	Current Value of Savings and Investments										
Age	25,000	40,000	50,000	75,000	100,000	125,000	150,000	175,000	200,000	225,000	250,000
35	26,972	43,154	53,943	80,915	107,886	134,858	161,829	188,801	215,772	242,744	269,716
40	17,660	28,255	35,319	52,979	70,638	88,298	105,958	123,617	141,277	158,937	176,596
45	11,563	18,500	23,125	34,688	46,251	57,813	69,376	80,938	92,501	104,064	115,626
50	7,571	12,113	15,141	22,712	30,283	37,853	45,424	52,994	60,565	68,136	75,706
55	4,957	7,931	9,914	14,871	19,827	24,784	29,741	34,698	39,655	44,612	49,569
60	3,245	5,193	6,491	9,737	12,982	16,228	19,473	22,719	25,964	29,210	32,455

Note: Estimated annual investment income assumes no additional investments; hypothetical
8.5% fixed rate of return, compounded monthly; estimated payout at retirement is from interest income only, at an average hypothetical 8.5% fixed rate of return, with no declining
principal; and retirement at age 65. This rate is for illustration purposes only and is not representative of the rate of return of a particular product. Rates of return may fluctuate over time.

5. Now, simply add up lines 2, 3, and 4 to arrive at
   your total estimated annual income at retirement.
   This is an estimate based upon the stated assump-
   tions, and actual income levels will vary based
   upon a variety of factors. _____

6. Finally, to calculate the gap between estimates of
   what you will need and what you will have when
   you retire, simply subtract the amount on line 5
   from the amount on line 1. _____

7. To determine the estimated investment amount
   that must be accumulated by retirement in order
   to generate sufficient income to bridge the annual
   income gap at age 65, divide line 6 by .085. _____

Note: This example again assumes an 8.5% rate of return, which is not representative of the
rate of return of a particular product but simply for illustration purposes. The effect of taxes
has not been considered in any example.

If there is a gap between what you will need and what you will have,
you must take steps immediately to close that gap. This is merely an
example that assumes you wish to retire at age 65 with a standard of
living similar to your current one. Your actual goals may include reaching

financial independence at an earlier age with more or less income than you are currently receiving.

Your Blueprint

At this point, you may be saying, "I see the points you are making and that I must change the way I think about money and the way I invest it." That's a good start, but at the same time you are probably saying to yourself (although you will not admit it to others), "I know little about investing, and I haven't a clue how to invest my money to achieve a balance between safety and prudent risk. I don't know how much money to invest, when to invest it, and what type of investment vehicles will best suit my needs."

Fortunately, there is a way to steer through this confusing maze of issues. You can do it by referring to a document, already in your hands, that can provide a blueprint for a financial plan customized for your income, assets, goals, and objectives. This document, as we have told you, is your federal tax return. It is the touchstone of our approach to financial planning and wealth creation.

The tax return provides a snapshot of your financial status. It tells how much money you make, the source of that money, the nature and value of your assets, and the percentage of your earnings that are eaten up by taxes. You can learn all of this from the quickest glimpse at your tax return. But the more you look, the more you learn. By studying your return carefully, you can gain invaluable insights into your spending habits, your investment discipline, whether or not you are taking advantage of tax-deferred vehicles allowed by the government, whether or not you are going to enjoy a comfortable retirement (if you remain on your current course), and if you are paying too much of your earnings to Uncle Sam and your state tax collectors. The tax return can tell you succinctly what you are doing right, what you are doing wrong, and the opportunities you are missing in managing (or, more often, *mis*managing) your personal finances. And most important, the tax return provides a blueprint for planning and building a successful money management program.

Beginning with Chapter 3, we move through the federal tax return Form 1040 line by line to show you how to use the document to build your financial plan. But first, it is important for you to understand our basic strategies for successful investing.

Chapter 2

Strategies for Successful Investing

> There is only one success—to be able to spend your life in your own way.
>
> Christopher Morley

The idea of investing in the stock market frightens a lot of people. And nothing engenders more fear than the thought of a stock market "crash."

Few people realize that it is possible to make your investments virtually "crash-proof"—that is, highly resistant to the cyclical ups and downs that keep many from investing in the market.

Crash-proof investing may sound like a pipe dream, but it isn't, *if* you use the basic investment principles outlined in this chapter.

Simply put, our investment principles are as follows:

10 Principles for Successful Investing

1. *Self-discipline,* not income level, determines your ability to save money.
2. If your "safe" investments don't *outpace inflation,* then your investments are not truly safe.
3. *Don't try to "time"* the stock market; those who do so usually fail.
4. Your investments should be part of an *overall strategy* designed to achieve your specific financial objectives.
5. Substantial growth of assets over the long term requires some *equity investments,* which can be volatile. The percentage of equities in your portfolio should be compatible with your tolerance for risk.
6. The most efficient portfolios are *properly diversified,* both within and among the basic asset categories.

7. The most successful investors are patient, *long-term* investors.
8. Investing should be as *systematic* as paying a monthly bill.
9. You should take a *holistic approach* to your financial life, recognizing that tax strategies, insurance needs, and investment goals are interrelated.
10. You should find a knowledgeable *tax and financial advisor* you can trust.

Most of these principles will be examined in detail in this chapter. They also provide a foundation for our discussions of various topics throughout the book.

Your Investment Options

When you stop to examine your investment options—from CDs to bonds to common stocks to stock options—you will quickly discover a fundamental truth about investing: You have the potential to earn higher returns in the long run by investing in those assets that demonstrate greater volatility. This truth raises two important questions: How much additional return should you expect to earn for bearing a greater risk, and How can that risk be minimized?

The first question introduces the concept of *risk premium*, the financial bonus an investor should expect over and above fixed-return assets (such as Treasury bills, notes, or bonds) as compensation for accepting the increased risk of equities or other assets that don't guarantee a specific return.

The second question introduces the concept of *risk-reward ratio*—the level of volatility you must tolerate to achieve an anticipated return. You will discover in this chapter that there are proven methods of dramatically reducing the risk in an investment portfolio, thereby improving the risk-reward ratio to levels acceptable even to the most conservative investors. Yes, even to you.

"Crashes Do Happen."

The fact is, most people invest on the basis of fear rather than on the basis of knowledge. They avoid equity investments, in particular, because they fear disasters—such as the mother of all disasters, a stock market crash. "Crashes do happen," they say. "There were big ones in 1929 and 1987, and another could occur tomorrow."

Although this is true, does that mean you stay away from the stock market? Let us answer that question with another question: Has the market recovered after both crashes? Yes, it has. Now let's ask another question: Has the market climbed ultimately to record highs after the crashes? Yes, again.

Naturally, you can always find reasons not to invest in the stock market. People use all sorts of excuses not to invest, but history shows that such rationalizations are rarely, if ever, justified.

To illustrate, let's examine a few past crises that frightened investors away from the market and look at the long-term results for those who continued to invest. The following examples are based on the performance of the Standard & Poor's 500 Index and assume reinvestment of all dividends:

* In 1960 a Communist government took over Cuba, only 90 miles away from the U.S. mainland. But an investor who put $10,000 in a wide range of common stocks that year and reinvested all dividends would have an investment now worth more than $175,865. That is a hefty 1,658% in growth.

* The prime rate soared to 8.5% in 1970, an unprecedented level two decades ago. Yet the same $10,000 invested in common stocks that year would be worth more than $82,893 today. That is growth of almost 729%.

* In 1980, Iran was holding 144 U.S. captives, and many people held on to their money. Those who parted with $10,000 to put in common stocks would have an investment worth over $46,961 today, racking up more than 360% in growth.

Exhibit 2-1 details the performance of stocks, bonds, and bills compared to inflation over the six decades from 1925 to 1992. As you study the chart, think of any war, economic crisis, natural disaster, or political upheaval that occurred during this period—Pearl Harbor, Watergate, the energy crisis, Vietnam. Note how the market responded to each of these crises: In every case, it resumed its growth.

There is an even more compelling reason not to be afraid of the stock market: The same market declines that may have prompted you to shy away from stocks actually present excellent buying opportunities. And that's precisely what the savviest investors do in times of concern and decline: They continue buying. Because they recognize that equities consistently outpace other investments and that today's stock bargains will appreciate dramatically in the coming months or years.

At this point, you are probably thinking, "I now realize the wisdom of investing in the stock market. But when is the best time for *me* to invest?" The answer is now—right away—don't wait. The longer the period between the time an investment is made and the time the money is needed to fund retirement or other long-term goal, the more the savvy investor will have to live on and enjoy.

Exhibit 2-1. Six-decade performance of stocks, bonds, and bills compared to inflation.

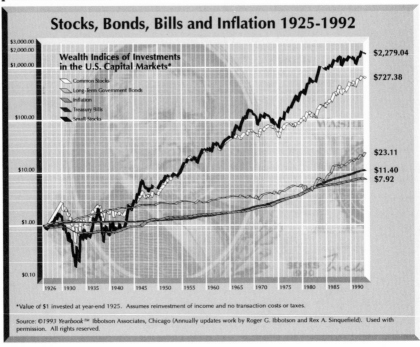

Stocks, Bonds, Bills and Inflation 1925-1992

Wealth Indices of Investments in the U.S. Capital Markets*

- Common Stocks
- Long-Term Government Bonds
- Inflation
- Treasury Bills
- Small Stocks

$2,279.04
$727.38
$23.11
$11.40
$7.92

*Value of $1 invested at year-end 1925. Assumes reinvestment of income and no transaction costs or taxes.

Source: ©1993 Yearbook™ Ibbotson Associates, Chicago (Annually updates work by Roger G. Ibbotson and Rex A. Sinquefield). Used with permission. All rights reserved.

Our approach is not to time the market, but instead to invest in quality securities for the long term. Even a cursory review of the market's history shows that like the tortoise in Aesop's fable, the patient, long-term market investor wins in the end. Buying and holding common stocks are the surest means by which the small investor can preserve and build wealth over the long term.

Successful investing really is that simple. It is so simple, in fact, that few people believe it can work. But it does.

EXAMPLE: Take the hypothetical case of sextuplets. Each brother receives an inheritance of $30,000. The first brother, Tim, starts investing his money, $2,000 a year, at age 30. Each of the five remaining brothers delays the start of investment by one year, in sequence. The last brother, Tipper, waits until age 35 to begin investing his $30,000. Each brother puts all of his money into the same mutual fund.

Tim, who had 35 years to build wealth, comes out ahead, with a value of $675,947. The next brother, with 34 years, has a portfolio valued at $608,940. The third brother's $30,000 investment is worth less, $548,083, after 33 years. Tipper, at the end of the line, manages to accumulate only $395,584 because he had only 30 years to save.

Waiting just six years cost $280,363. While the sextuplets may be fictitious, the numbers are based on the historical performance of an actual equity mutual fund. These numbers, of course, cannot indicate the future performance of any investment.

As the example of the hypothetical sextuplets clearly shows, the longer investing is delayed, the less money is available for future financial needs. Investing early puts time to work for you and makes it possible to build a much greater base of wealth.

The shocking truth about those just starting their careers today is that 87% of them will be forced to retire on an income of less than $10,000 a year. Of those just starting out, 46% will live on less than $5,000 a year during retirement. None of these people plan to retire poor; the tragedy is that they fail to plan at all. You, however, need not become a part of these statistics.

Those who invest on the basis of knowledge and experience rather than fear consistently profit in the stock market. They do so by looking beyond immediate ups and downs in stock prices, basing their actions instead on the long-term perspective, grounded in history, that equities will continue to grow—outpacing inflation, bank accounts, certificates of deposit, and most other investments.

If this thinking seems rational enough but you are still wary of moving from "safe" investments to equities, why not make a gradual transition? Move 10–20% of your safe money out of low-yielding CDs and into a carefully structured mutual fund portfolio (just what a mutual fund is, and how to select one, is discussed later in this chapter). Establish a reasonable time frame for gauging the performance of this investment. As you grow comfortable with your new investments, and as the return on your money rises over time, shift more of your assets in 20% increments from CDs to mutual funds.

If history is any guide, you will be taking a major step toward achieving financial freedom.

Diversification

The key to investing with confidence is knowledge. Rather than invest haphazardly in a patchwork of securities, optimize your risk-reward ratio through the careful selection of an investment portfolio. The proper choice of investments creates an element of diversification that stabilizes your portfolio in changing economic climates.

To better understand the benefits of diversification, imagine you are boarding an elevator with six supporting cables. Each of those six cables can easily hold the weight of the elevator, thus ensuring a safe ride. If one of the cables breaks, clearly the likelihood of a safe ride decreases, but you are not in immediate jeopardy. And if another cable breaks, and then still another, the danger grows, but there are still remaining cables to protect you. The odds of all the cables breaking, causing the elevator to come crashing down, are almost nil.

The safety provided by the elevator's multiple cables is similar to the safety provided by a diversified mix of assets in a portfolio. If one or two investments lag behind, the other investments in the balanced portfolio are designed to provide a strong measure of safety and a steady return.

Even where investment "cables" break, a diversified portfolio will likely produce a higher return than the "safest" investment with an indestructible cable.

EXAMPLE: Kathleen Johnson, at age 40, has $100,000 to invest and wants to retire by age 65. Were Kathleen to take the super-safe route, investing the entire sum in a 5% certificate of deposit, she would have $338,635 by retirement age before taxes, assuming she reinvested all the interest in 5% CDs.

On the other hand, Kathleen might diversify her portfolio. She invests $20,000 in stock options, only to lose the entire amount. She puts $20,000 in precious metals, but the investment simply returns her capital without any additional income. She invests $20,000 in 6.5% tax-free bonds, $20,000 in blue-chip stocks that average a 10% return, and $20,000 in growth stocks that produce a 12% return. Even with these decidedly mixed results, her $100,000 grows to $673,249.

Asset Allocation

"But wait," you say. "How can you guarantee that some of Kathleen Johnson's assets will perform well, while others will not? Couldn't all her investments fail?"

Now is a good time for you to learn about a concept called asset allocation. Let's start by looking at how the major categories of assets have fared during consecutive periods of inflation, recession, and growth*:

---

*This information, adapted from H. D. Vest's 1993 Asset Allocation Study, assesses the period from 1977 to 1985, defining 1977–1979 as an inflationary period, 1980–1982 as a recessionary period, and 1983–1985 as a growth period.

A **growth period** is defined as a period during which GNP growth exceeds the rate of inflation. An **inflationary period** is a period during which the inflation

Asset Category	Growth	Inflation	Recession
Large–cap equities	Excellent	Poor	Excellent
Small-cap equities	Excellent	Excellent	Excellent
Fixed income	Excellent	Poor	Good
International	Excellent	Excellent	Poor
Precious metals	Poor	Excellent	Excellent
Real estate	Excellent	Excellent	Excellent
Energy	Excellent	Good	Poor

While this chart does not reflect how different asset categories will perform in every economic cycle, it does illustrate the point that some asset classes thrive in economic climates where others falter. The predictability of such relationships over the long term is critical to our balanced approach to investing.

By carefully spreading investments among the six major asset categories—common stocks (including large-cap and small-cap equities), bonds, international stocks and bonds, real estate, precious metals, and energy—you can achieve a level of diversification that can make you far more comfortable with market investing.

Although the concept of asset allocation may be new to you, it is anything but a new idea. Indeed, the fundamental concept is as old as ancient Hebrew scripture. As the Talmud advises, "Let every man divide his money into three parts, and invest a third in land, a third in business, and a third let him keep in reserve."

Recent studies have presented persuasive evidence that an investor's long-term asset allocation decision does far more to influence long-term

---

rate exceeds GNP growth. A period of **recession** is a period during which GNP growth is negative.

For our purposes, performance of an asset class is "excellent" when it outpaces inflation by more than 5 percentage points, "good" when it outpaces inflation by 1–5 percentage points, and "poor" when it fails to outpace inflation by at least one percentage point.

Large cap equities, or common stocks of large companies, are represented by the Standard & Poor 500 Index. **Small cap equities,** or common stocks of small companies, are defined as the smallest 20% of companies on the New York Stock Exchange based on market capitalization. **Energy** is represented by the S&P Oil Composite Index; **fixed income,** by a compilation of Salomon Brothers' Long-Term Corporate Bond Index and Government Bond Index; **international,** by Morgan Stanley Capital International—Europe, Australia, and Far East (EAFE); and **Real Estate,** by the National Association of Real Estate Investment Trusts Equity Index. **Precious metals** is represented by a composite of precious metals mutual funds.

portfolio returns and risk than do decisions concerning security selection and market timing.

The specific combination of assets that is right for you depends on your investment goals, tolerance for risk, and time frame. Regardless of the mix of assets in your portfolio, however, our underlying concept is that your investments should work in harmony, with the various components performing differently under varying economic conditions.

The Sharpe Ratio

As we have indicated before, when comparing alternative asset classes for investment, in the long run you will generally earn higher returns by investing in those assets that demonstrate greater volatility. The question is, How can you build a portfolio that maximizes your **risk premium** (or the additional return you should expect over and above those of risk-free assets) per unit of risk?

You may have seen the term **historical standard deviation** (a measure of investment volatility) or heard of risk premium statistics before. By themselves, these numbers are rarely useful; even comparing these statistics among various asset categories is of limited use. However, the statistics are quite meaningful when combined to create a measure of risk and trade-off such as the so-called **Sharpe ratio.**

Created by Dr. William Sharpe, this ratio is a statistic comprised of standard deviation and risk premium. It helps investors relate the level of risk incurred to achieve marginal increases in returns when comparing two or more alternative investments. The Sharpe ratio is computed by dividing the risk premium of an asset class by the standard deviation of that asset class.

To illustrate the benefits of asset allocation, we simulated the performance of a simple portfolio comprised of investments in the six major asset categories. We compared the performance of this "base portfolio" to the performance of individual asset types over a 20-year period. Exhibit 2-2 summarizes the results of that simulation.*

---

*This simulation assumed that $1 was invested on January 1, 1970, in a "base portfolio" that was allocated evenly to each of the following six asset categories (i.e., one-sixth allocation or about $0.17 to each category): long-term U.S. government bonds, natural resources and energy stocks, blue-chip stocks, real estate investment trusts, international stocks, and precious metal stocks. We further assumed that on December 31 of each year for the 20-year period ending December 31, 1989, the portfolio was automatically rebalanced to its original one-sixth strategic asset allocation mix. That is, those asset categories whose values exceeded their one-sixth allocation due to reinvested dividends, interest, and appreciation

This research reaffirms the idea that disciplined allocation of assets among the major asset categories significantly increases portfolio returns while greatly minimizing portfolio risk. The base portfolio (diversified) has the highest Sharpe ratio, and its internal rate of return during this period exceeds all other asset categories except precious metals stocks, which are far more volatile.

The key point here is that solid, long-term wealth accumulation requires that you resist the temptation of such emotional investing as, say, limiting yourself to safe investments or rushing helter-skelter from one hot investment idea to another. Over the years, a carefully structured, diversified portfolio will, in the vast majority of cases, produce the greatest returns, thus helping you to achieve financial independence.

The Mutual Fund

One of the cornerstones of our approach to achieving financial freedom is to simplify the investment process so that you can understand and oversee your investments. We want you to be able to make sense out of the seemingly confusing maze of investment options. At the same time, we want your money to benefit from sophisticated management so that it can generate superior returns on a consistent basis.

For most people, these goals can be best achieved by investing in

Exhibit 2-2. Comparison of base portfolio to asset classes (1970–1989).

	Internal Rate of Return %	Avg. Annual Return %	Standard Deviation %	Sharpe Ratio
BASE PORTFOLIO	14.65	15.35	12.87	0.60
Blue Chip Stocks	11.55	12.84	16.34	0.32
Small Stocks	13.64	16.26	23.85	0.36
Long-term Gov't Bonds	9.01	9.60	11.76	0.16
Int'l Stocks	14.30	16.67	22.51	0.40
Real Estate Inv. Trusts	12.54	13.58	15.00	0.40
Precious Metals Stocks	18.32	26.59	51.76	0.37
Energy Stocks	11.72	13.57	20.58	0.29
Treasury Bills	7.59	7.62	2.62	.02
Consumer Price Index	5.99	6.05	3.60	N/A

were sold off to the one-sixth limit and the proceeds invested in the underperforming asset categories.

mutual funds. Put simply, mutual funds are investment pools managed by professionals. The type and the quality of the instruments that make up the investment pools vary depending on the category of fund and the specific fund in the category.

Mutual funds give individual investors the power of numbers. Assume you have $1,000 to invest in corporate bonds and you purchase one ABC Co. bond for that sum. Even if ABC is a stellar company, it is clear that you have no diversification and are thus totally dependent on ABC's fate. On the other hand, if you pool your $1,000 with 999 investors seeking similar objectives, you will have $1 million among you, enabling the group to purchase 1,000 bonds, thus spreading the risk and the opportunity for income and appreciation over a broad range of companies and industries. And with $1 million to spend, the group could afford to hire a professional to make buy/sell decisions on its behalf. This, in a nutshell, is how a mutual fund works. It gives even small investors the opportunity to invest in markets the way million-dollar investors do.

One appealing feature of mutual fund investing is that the choices at your disposal are virtually unlimited. Among the great family of mutual funds are those investing in blue-chip stocks, small-company stocks, stocks of overseas companies, and corporate bonds, as well as hybrids of various investments.

Perhaps most important, mutual funds offer built-in diversification. An equity mutual fund, for example, cannot invest more than 5% of its money in any one company, nor can it own more than 10% of the outstanding shares of any single company. Instead, fund managers typically spread their investments over a substantial portfolio of securities, providing diversification within a certain type of investment vehicle (such as stocks or bonds).

The best way for you to achieve the ideal mix of risk and reward, however, is to go a step further, by building a diversified portfolio of two or more mutual funds that invest in different asset classes. This type of investment, committed for the long term, is the key to crash-proof investing.

Here are four additional advantages to investing in mutual funds:

1. *Professional management.* Having professionals skilled in analyzing and buying various securities do your investing for you is a much wiser course than investing on the basis of tips or hunches. Even if you have the ability to analyze securities and to select those with favorable prospects, you don't live with the markets on a daily basis. Therefore, you may overlook the events or trends that signal the need to make a change in your investments. Fund managers are in a position to do so on your behalf.

2. *Liquidity.* Funds are obligated to redeem shares promptly; redemption requests are processed within seven days. In most cases, you can arrange to have your money much sooner. Should a fund have check-writing privileges, you can have instant access to your money. And if a bank wire feature is offered (as it is by most mutual funds), your money can be wired to your bank account within a few days.

3. *Timely distributions.* Distributions of dividends and interest are generally made monthly, and capital gains, annually. These sums can be taken as cash or automatically reinvested, thus accelerating the buildup of values in your fund.

4. *Flexibility.* Investments can generally be transferred from one type of fund (blue-chip stocks or money markets) to another type of fund (small-company stocks or high-yield bonds) within the same family of funds. This allows you to switch investments according to how you think the economic climate will favor one strategy over another, or as your personal needs evolve.

The Safety Trap

"Hold on," you may be saying. "If mutual funds invest in stocks and bonds, they can't be safe!" If that's what you think, you have fallen into the fatal trap of so-called riskless investing. Why is that a trap? Because there are no such things as riskless investments. Sure there are bank accounts and certificates of deposit guaranteed by the federal government, but is *guaranteed* the same as *riskless?* The answer is no. When you limit all or most of your money to "safe" investments, you are trading away the opportunity to gain significant capital appreciation (as afforded by stocks) in return for the illusion of safety.

We say the *illusion* of safety because investments that are limited to low or mediocre yields (as is generally the case with bank accounts and CDs) are subject to the ravages of inflation. When inflation outpaces the earnings on your money, the purchasing power of so-called safe investments withers away. Viewed in this real world context, does that sound safe to you? Absolutely not.

If the idea of taking money out of CDs and investing the proceeds in mutual funds leaves you unnerved, consider a process that makes your mutual fund look more like a CD. This will help to make you comfortable with the investment and at the same time give you the potential for superior financial performance.

The strategy is geared toward those who wish to draw regular income from their investments. It works this way: From your mutual fund, take a systematic withdrawal that is less than the regular distribution rate. For example, if you are in a low tax bracket, you might select a "plain vanilla" government bond fund yielding 7%. Instead of taking the entire yield, set up a systematic withdrawal based on 6%.

Look at what this strategy accomplishes: Your return likely exceeds that of CDs by at least a percentage point. Your monthly checks will remain the same. Even if the mutual fund changes the distribution, you will receive a constant sum under the systematic withdrawal plan. In addition, the principal will continue to grow because a small percentage is being reinvested each month. Although it is true that the value of the fund will rise and fall, with reinvestment it should continue to grow.

In many cases, systematic withdrawals from a mutual fund can give a cautious investor seeking appreciation the best of all worlds: relative peace of mind, the potential for principal to grow, and liquidity.

Which Funds Are Best for You

Before you embark on a mutual fund investment program, two critical factors must be addressed: how much money you have to invest and how many years you have to achieve your financial objectives (college education, retirement, down payment for a home).

Let's take them one at a time. If you have $10,000 or less, you will want to concentrate your modest investment, at most, in two mutual funds. This enables you to take a meaningful position in a limited number of funds that are likely to perform well for you. Stepping up to investment sums of greater than $10,000 enables you to achieve greater diversification, seeding your money into a portfolio of up to six asset classes.

The other key factor to consider, investment time frame, stresses the need to link your investment strategy to your time horizon. If you have a short-term objective of less than three years, your investment options are limited to certificates of deposit and money market funds. These vehicles are recommended because you do not have time to ride out fluctuations in the higher-yielding but less stable markets.

For objectives of from three to five years, you can begin to accept a bit more risk in return for the reward of higher returns. Consider adding to the investment mix of CDs and money market funds, short-term U.S. government securities funds, and, if you are in a high tax bracket, tax-exempt municipal bond trusts or funds. For objectives of more than five years, returns can be enhanced through the use of a wide range of investment vehicles. Consider diversifying your portfolio to include investments in stocks (of U.S. and international companies), bonds, real estate, precious metals, and energy.

Your mutual fund investments can be purchased and monitored with the assistance of a tax and financial professional, who can identify the ideal mix of investment options for your personal needs, goals, and risk tolerance and provide you with regular reports on the portfolio's performance.

Types of Mutual Funds

Recognizing that a sound portfolio is always based on diversification, let's review some of the major types of mutual funds that can be included in your asset mix.

Fixed-Income Funds

Fixed-income funds are typically pools of U.S. government obligations, municipal obligations, or corporate bonds. The fund manager's primary objective is to provide a sizeable and stable flow of investment income to the shareholders.

A key attribute of these funds is that the share price fluctuates inversely with interest rates. Therefore, as interest rates decline, the value of the debt instruments rises.

For example, assume you invest in a bond fund with a current yield of 7%. Should interest rates rise to 8%, the price of the mutual fund shares will decline because higher yields are easily available outside of the fund. But the reverse is also true. If interest rates drop to 6%, the price of the shares will increase, because the fund offers a higher yield than prevailing rates.

Historically, the bond market has performed best during periods of economic growth or deflation. In these times, debt is attractive because of its relative inherent safety and because of its characteristic of producing current income.

Government Securities Funds. There are three major kinds of fixed-income funds: government securities funds, municipal funds, and corporate funds.

Government securities funds may consist of a pool of U.S. government securities, including T-bills, long-term notes and bonds, and government agency issues. Although such funds are not insured, the fact that the securities are backed by the faith and credit of the U.S. government virtually eliminates the risk of default, thus making these funds among the safest available in terms of principal.

Advantages of Investing in Fixed-Income Mutual Funds

+ Less fluctuation of principal (as compared to equities)
+ Stable income stream
+ Tax-free income (available in some funds)

Disadvantages of Investing in Fixed-Income Mutual Funds

− Price volatility (as compared to money market funds)
− Default risk (some of the bond issuers could default)
− Drop in yield, especially in a short-term fixed income fund,
  if fund managers are forced to replace retiring bonds with
  low-yielding replacements

There is, however, a risk of principal fluctuation. Because government bond prices react inversely to interest rates more than any other investment, the price of the portfolio (and therefore the investor's principal) will fluctuate with market rates. The mitigating factor is that fund managers account for this, taking steps to try to maintain a stable net asset value. Government funds are suitable for conservative investors seeking current income with safety of principal. Usually, these funds are purchased by those investors who need a safe and secure investment.

Municipal Bond Funds. Municipal bond funds seek high current income that is free from federal taxation—and in some cases, exempt from state and local income taxes as well.

Although the yields on municipal bond funds may be lower than the yields available through taxable funds, any comparison of these investments must account for the impact of taxation. This means calculating a tax-free fund's taxable equivalent yield—or the amount of yield you would have to obtain from a taxable instrument to equal the yield from a tax-free fund. This can be accomplished through this equation:

$$\frac{\text{current yield}}{1.00 - \text{investor's marginal tax rate.}}$$

So if you are in the 28% tax bracket, an investment in municipal bonds yielding 6% before tax would have a tax-equivalent yield of 8.3%. A taxable bond fund would have to offer a yield of more than 8.3% to give you a better return.

Municipal bond funds are recommended vehicles for conservative individuals in high tax brackets who seek current tax-free income.

Corporate Bond Funds. Corporate bond funds invest in debt securities such as corporate bonds and debentures, convertible bonds, notes, or commercial paper. In general, these funds offer higher yields than government bond funds.

Corporate bond funds fall into two primary categories:

1. *High-quality funds.* These funds invest in corporate bonds carrying the top four bond ratings (AAA, AA, A, or BBB by Standard & Poor; Aaa, Aa, A, and Baa by Moody). In terms of safety of principal, these blue-chip bond funds are considered second only to U.S. government and muni bond funds. For this reason, they are recommended for conservative investors who seek to combine current income and safety of principal.

2. *High-yield funds.* These funds invest in low-grade, high-yield corporate bonds as well as preferred and common stock. Considering that the lower grade of the bonds (generally BBB/Baa or below) implies a higher risk, so too is the yield higher than blue-chip yields.

High-yield corporate bond funds are for investors who seek a high current income, with stability of principal as a secondary concern.

Equity Funds

Just as fixed-income funds are comprised of various kinds of bonds, equity funds are invested in shares of corporate common stock. In general, equities offer the opportunity for greater returns than bonds, but at a higher risk.

Historically, equities have produced the highest long-term returns, particularly during periods of economic growth, when interest rates are maintained at reasonable levels. The reason for this is simple: When financing is relatively inexpensive, a company is in a position to borrow money to expand operations and to increase production, boosting its dividends and raising the value and price of its stock. Investments in equity mutual funds can appreciate dramatically in this type of economic environment.

Nevertheless, you should not necessarily rush to make equity funds the bulk of your portfolio. Remember, diversification is the foundation of our investment approach. Because every investment vehicle has its share of risks and/or negative factors, you should never overload on any single investment type or product.

For example, when the economy is lagging, equity funds may fare poorly compared to safer, slow-and-steady options such as government bond funds. However, when a portfolio is properly balanced, the various investment components work in an integrated fashion to protect against severe losses. When one component of the portfolio declines, another may rise, thus maintaining a high level of value in the account.

It all depends on you. What risk-reward ratio are you comfortable with—not only financially, but psychologically? Would temporary fluctuations of principal send you into a panic? Too often, panicky investors sell stock at just the wrong time.

Depending on your own risk tolerance, we recommend that U.S. equity mutual funds (as opposed to international funds, which we will discuss later) comprise one of the following percentage ranges in your portfolio:

Cautious investors and those over age 55:	20–25%
Investors, generally between ages 35 and 55, who are comfortable with moderate levels of risk:	25–35%
Aggressive investors, generally between ages 25 and 35, willing to accept more risk for the opportunity to achieve higher returns:	40% or more

---

Advantages of Investing in Equity Funds

+ Higher overall return (than bonds or other options based on historical figures)
+ More growth potential than with debt instruments
+ Highest total return during economic growth

Disadvantages of Investing in Equity Funds

− Greater risk than fixed-income funds
− More price volatility than fixed-income funds
− In case of corporate insolvency, payment to equity shareholders after bondholders

---

Within the universe of domestic equity funds, you can achieve added diversification—and in the process precisely target your investment objectives—by spreading assets among the major kinds of funds in this category.

The following are three types of equity funds, in order of increasing risk—and potential reward:

1. *Growth and income funds.* These funds invest primarily in blue-chip stocks—the bedrock of the corporate community, including the nation's oldest and largest companies. Although all equity investing is exposed to some price volatility, historically these quality issues tend to regain their value after weak markets and to maintain continued growth over the years. For this reason, blue chips should be included in most portfolios, with a higher percentage of these funds allocated for older and/or more conservative investors.

2. *Growth funds.* As the name implies, growth funds invest in common stocks that are likely to achieve substantial capital growth. Although stocks in this group are generally issued by high-quality companies, they need not be as mature or as stable as blue chips. On the positive side, they may be able to achieve faster and more impressive growth than the bluest of the blues.

3. *Aggressive growth funds.* These are at the opposite end of the risk/reward ratio from the blue chips. Investments are concentrated in companies that for one reason or another are thought to be good candidates for strong and/or rapid capital appreciation.

Favored stocks among aggressive growth funds are small companies with promising products or technologies, companies that have suffered fiscal setbacks but that are turnaround prospects, and other companies that appear to be exceptional bargains because they are selling well below book value.

In recent years, aggressive growth stock funds specializing in small companies have outperformed virtually every other type of mutual fund. This exceptional return, however, must be viewed in the context of the funds' greater volatility and higher risk. For this reason, such funds are best suited to investors willing to take a bit of a gamble.

Balanced Funds

Balanced Funds are hybrids of fixed-income and equity funds. In order to achieve a "balanced" investment portfolio, the managers of these funds invest in a mix of stocks and debt obligations. This blend of securities is designed to produce current income (from the debt instruments) and long-term capital appreciation (from the stocks) while maintaining relative safety of principal.

Generally, fund managers have the discretion to shift dollars from debt to equity components, and even to cash positions, based on their view of market conditions. This flexibility can make these funds more stable than pure equity funds. Typically, the fund managers will move out of equities in bear markets.

A balanced fund could be an excellent choice for you if your resources available for investing are less than $5,000 and you are unable to spread out over different types of funds. However, even people with money invested in several funds sometimes choose balanced funds as a means of securing relative safety with growth potential.

Advantages of Investing in Balanced Funds

+ More conservative than pure equity investments because bond instruments reduce principal risk
+ High security of principal coupled with current income and capital appreciation over the long run
+ Less volatility than pure equity funds

Disadvantages of Investing in Balanced Funds

− More aggressive than fixed-income funds, thus increasing the risk of capital fluctuation
− Lower long-term growth than pure equity funds

Specialty Funds

Specialty funds are among the lesser known and underutilized members of the mutual fund universe. Because these funds can provide effective vehicles for boosting the value and/or the stability of your investment portfolio, you should make it a point to develop a working knowledge of them.

Sector Funds. These funds concentrate their investments in a market niche, most commonly a particular industry such as health care, biotechnology, utilities, chemicals, or financial services. The idea behind these funds is to direct a segment of your portfolio toward an industry you believe will experience superior growth.

For example, if you are fascinated with transportation, read extensively about the companies in that industry, and believe they will perform exceptionally well, you may want to place as much as 5% of your assets into a transportation sector fund. Because you are exposed to the cyclical swings of a single industry, there are greater risks here than in general equity funds. Thus the reason to limit your investment in these niche funds.

Oil and Energy Funds. These are actually sector funds, but we treat them separately because they should have a place in every balanced portfolio, primarily as an inflation hedge.

These funds invest in the stocks of oil and other energy-related companies. The major reason for their importance is that oil, much like real estate, historically correlates negatively with stocks and bonds. That's because oil performance is generally linked less to the current status of the U.S. economy than to such external factors as OPEC pricing.

On the other hand, oil is correlated positively with consumer prices. This means investors can look to oil investments to offset rising consumer prices driven, in part, by increases in energy prices.

Oil and energy funds should account for 5–10% of your total portfolio.

Money Market Funds. Money markets are the most popular of specialty funds. They concentrate their investments in large-denomination, short-term money market instruments. Typically, money market funds are used to park cash for short periods of time as it is moved from one investment to another. Money market funds are also useful as a safe, stable haven for funds that will be needed in less than three years.

Money market funds offer yields that are generally similar to bank short-term CD rates, offer instant liquidity (including check-writing privileges), and provide for stable principal. Shares are purchased and sold at a fixed price of $1 each; earnings accrue from the yields paid by the funds.

Gold Funds. Gold funds are generally used as an inflation hedge and a safe haven in times of political and economic uncertainty. Because gold (and other precious metals) can fare well when stocks and bonds are staggering, they should figure into a well-balanced portfolio, representing 5–10% of your total investment dollars.

Typically, gold mutual funds make investments in gold bullion, South African gold stocks, or non-South African gold stocks. To diversify within the precious metals category, it is a good idea to spread your investment into at least two of these most common types of funds (while keeping the total investment to 5–10% of your portfolio).

International Funds. These have moved from a once-obscure investment option to a critical component of the well-balanced portfolio that should account for 20–25% of your investment dollars (if you are a defensive investor), or 25–30% if you are inclined to be more aggressive.

The importance of international funds (or funds that invest in the stocks of foreign countries) to your portfolio stems from three factors:

1. An increasing number of today's fastest-growing and best-managed companies are located outside of the United States. By including them in your portfolio, you benefit from their prosperity and continued growth prospects.
2. These funds assure you of economic diversification through investment in overseas economies. For example, a strong U.S. dollar will hurt the funds' performance, while a weaker dollar will likely prove beneficial to you as an investor in international funds.
3. Historically, international funds have fared well during periods of inflation. Because the performance of international stocks does not correlate closely with that of U.S. stocks and bonds, international investments are valuable for maintaining portfolio stability during varying economic conditions.

Small investors who wish to test the international waters may invest in a *global fund*, which invests in both domestic *and* foreign stocks.

Unit Investment Trusts

Now that you have a working knowledge of mutual funds and can begin to make decisions on the right mix of funds for your needs, you are well advised to learn about a similar type of investment, the **unit investment trust** (UIT).

Put simply, a UIT is a pool of individual securities, such as municipal bonds or other government obligations. When you purchase a unit of the trust, you are buying a portion of the pooled investments.

The most significant difference between a UIT and a mutual fund is that the former is not managed on an ongoing basis. The trust sponsor selects the investments that go into the UIT and ends his obligations there—as opposed to a mutual fund manager, who continually buys and sells investments for the fund.

The following are the two major types of UITs:

1. **Tax-free UITs** invest in portfolios of municipal bonds, typically diversified to encompass different municipalities, types of public projects being financed, and maturities (which generally range from 5 to 10 years for short-term bonds; 20 to 30 years for long-term bonds). For added safety, most UITs limit their holdings to bonds rated A or better by Moody or Standard & Poor.

2. **Taxable UITs** concentrate their investments in taxable securities. Although a wide range of stocks and bonds can be invested in the portfo-

lios, many of the trusts invest heavily in **Government National Mortgage Association (GNMA)** securities, commonly known as Ginnie Maes.

A GNMA security is composed of a pool of single-family residential mortgages, diversified by maturity and interest rates. When the homeowners holding the mortgages make their payments, the funds flow through to the owners of the GNMAs.

The investments offer a fixed rate of return made up of interest and principal on the mortgage payments. As principal is repaid, investors may want to keep reinvesting their money in order to maintain a high yield on their investment accounts.

In addition to Ginnie Maes, many taxable UITS invest heavily in corporate bonds, such as **first deed utility bonds.**

Regardless of the type of unit investment trust you choose, UITs share some common characteristics. For one thing, the housekeeping functions associated with owning individual securities are performed by the trust sponsor. This includes the safekeeping of securities and the collection of interest payments from the bond issuers. Ease of ownership, therefore, is a major plus.

The mix of securities in a trust remains constant. Once the portfolio of investments is assembled, the components do not change. The plus side of this is that there are no management fees; the minus side is that unlike mutual funds, there is no active management to update and change the mix of securities in the trust to accommodate for changing market conditions.

Investments in UITs are generally liquid. Once the initial shares have been sold, investors can often resell their units in a secondary market.

Typically, distributions of UIT interest and principal can be reinvested in the fund sponsor's mutual fund vehicles (including money market accounts) with little or no sales charge.

UIT values will fluctuate in tandem with prevailing market conditions. For example, if the prime interest rate rises, a UIT will likely decline in value; conversely, if the prime falls, the UIT's value may rise. Hence, liquidating a UIT before the maturity date may result in a capital gain or loss.

Are UITs right for your investment needs and temperament? The UIT offers so many positives for so many types of investors that the answer is probably yes. Let's begin with tax-free UITs; you may want to consider this vehicle if you find yourself in one or more of the following categories:

* Your high tax bracket leads you to seek investments that do not increase your taxable income.

* You seek a steady income stream to provide for monthly living expenses.
* You own individual municipal bonds and would benefit from professional selection of the appropriate bonds as well as gain wider diversification than what you could achieve on your own.
* You are seeking to trade up from low CD rates without incurring undue risk. Tax-free UITs may provide a higher equivalent yield than taxable CDs. What's more, you may be able to purchase insured UITs, thus achieving the safety of CDs while still trading up in yield.
* You are seeking a tax-exempt way to save for college. Under this approach, you purchase a tax-free UIT that is due to mature at or around the date tuition will have to be paid. Over the years, interest payments received from the trust are reinvested in tax-free mutual funds, thus keeping all of the dollars working toward your financial goal.

If you are seeking a tax-exempt means of saving for retirement, you can use a similar approach to the tuition program. Once you retire, however, the UIT income can be taken as monthly distributions rather than shifted into mutual funds.

Consider taxable UITs if you meet any of these tests:

* You have retired, are thus in a lower tax bracket, and want a steady stream of income.
* You want to add a conservative component to your investment portfolio, using the UITs to balance some of the higher-risk vehicles you now own.
* You are a conservative investor who takes comfort in the fact that GNMAs are guaranteed.

Before we move on, let's briefly recap the key differences between mutual funds and UITs:

1. *Fixed vs. open portfolio.* A UIT is a **fixed portfolio,** which means that securities can never be added once the portfolio is established. In contrast, mutual fund managers continually buy and sell the underlying securities with the goal of maximizing yield.
2. *Steady return vs. variable return.* UITs offer a steady stream of interest income at a fixed rate. Mutual fund yields can vary with

changes in the underlying issues and with changing market conditions.

3. *Known maturity vs. perpetual portfolio.* Each UIT portfolio matures when the principal of all the bonds held in it is distributed. In contrast, a fixed-income mutual fund can last forever.

4. *Repayment of principal.* As individual bonds within a UIT portfolio mature, the principal is repaid to you along with your regular interest payment. On the other hand, a mutual fund pays only dividends and capital gains earned from the investment.

Whatever investment option you believe is best for you, we recommend that you seek the advice of a tax and financial professional before making your choice.

Getting Help

Certainly you can develop and implement a financial plan without professional assistance, but if you do, your foundation of knowledge should go much deeper than the overview we have just provided.

Expert advice and assistance, we believe, is as vital to your long-term financial security as it is to your physical well-being. If a family member needed open-heart surgery, would you *even consider* performing the operation yourself? Would it matter to you if you had read a few books on the subject?

Similarly, you shouldn't take chances with your family's financial future. In addition to their expertise in securities, financial professionals also have the time to monitor your investments daily. And they can help you to set realistic and achievable financial goals for you and your family.

You can receive financial planning help from a variety of sources, including stockbrokers, insurance agents, attorneys, and professional money managers. Generally, stockbrokers and insurance agents are compensated by commissions. Professional money managers often receive fees based on a percentage of their clients' managed assets. Attorneys and some professional money managers charge hourly fees for their advice.

All these choices have their pros and cons. Overall, however, we believe the best person for the great majority of Americans to turn to for their financial planning needs is their family accountant or tax preparer— particularly if he or she is licensed to provide clients with the full range of investment products.

Your Tax Professional: The Optimal Choice

While brokers, lawyers, and others may be able to help you, there are three key advantages of turning to your tax professional for financial planning:

1. *Tax professionals have an intimate knowledge of their clients' financial situations.* The best financial services practitioners are knowledgeable about the financial world in general—and about your financial situation in particular. They are able to take a holistic approach to your finances, because they know about your specific needs.

For most Americans, an ideal fit in this area is the family tax professional who offers financial planning. Tax planning, as we have explained, is a vital part of a comprehensive approach to financial services. Financial planning and implementation always have tax consequences, which your tax professional is well-equipped to handle.

At the least, you should make sure your financial advisor is well aware of such consequences and knows how the tax laws will affect you individually. You want your financial program to solve problems rather than create new ones.

2. *Tax professionals are generally relationship- rather than transaction-oriented.* When you go to stockbrokers or insurance agents for financial planning advice, their primary motivation is to sell a particular financial product. That is because these advisors derive their income from commissions on the sale of stocks, bonds, mutual funds, insurance, and other products. Their expertise is generally in a specific product area.

Stockbrokers make money only when they sell stocks; insurance agents make money only by selling policies. Your specific financial needs may be a secondary concern. By contrast, a tax professional who adds financial planning to his or her practice has an opportunity to build on preexisting client relationships that are based on knowledge and trust.

Whether compensated by commissions or fees, tax professionals sit on the same side of the table as their clients when choosing an investment strategy. Strong client relationships are and always will be the tax professional's bread and butter.

3. *Tax professionals' planning services are affordable to the great majority of Americans.* Traditionally, it has been difficult for mainstream, working Americans to acquire professional help with their finances. Professional financial managers, who charge fees based on assets under management, often require that their clients own $100,000 or more in investable assets.

Other financial planners charge hourly fees of $100 or more to formulate generic investment programs that are often never implemented.

By integrating financial planning into their existing practices, tax professionals can offer informed investment advice to middle-income Americans.

Whomever you choose as an investment advisor, make sure the person is driven by your needs rather than some sales quota. Find someone you can trust, who knows you, and has studied your personal tax and financial situation.

*   *   *   *

And now it is time to look at Tax Form 1040 from an entirely new perspective, taking into account what the figures you enter mean for your financial strategy. We'll begin with the 1040's exemption section.

Chapter 3

Exemptions—What the Number You Enter Represents: Line 6

> Money is a good servant, but a bad master.
>
> French proverb

Most Americans view the exemptions line of Form 1040 as little more than an opportunity to take deductions for dependents. But when you think about it, the exemptions line opens a window into your financial needs, current and future.

Opening a Window

If you are claiming children, for example, have you considered what will happen to them when you die? Will they be able to afford a college education? If you will need an estimated $25,000 to $40,000 a year for college within 10 years, do you know how much money you must be saving and investing over this period to provide the necessary funds?

The point is, you must take steps now to maximize your family's financial well-being during your lifetime and after you pass away. This means reviewing your provisions for educational funding, disability and life insurance, parental or dependent care, and estate planning.

Life Insurance

Shrewd money management is defensive as well as offensive. Insurance is your means of protecting assets and earnings potential against the threat of death and other catastrophes.

Just as we use a systematic process of investing to build our upside potential in wealth creation, we must use insurance to protect against the downside risks that can, if left uncovered, wipe out a lifetime of financial gains.

If you list a spouse or children as dependents, consider whether you have adequate insurance to cover the wide range of perils they are exposed to. Consider first your need for life insurance. Do you have enough coverage? And do you have the appropriate type of insurance? Let's address these questions one at a time.

1. *"How much insurance do I need?"* The rule of thumb on coverage levels is that an individual needs at least enough of a death benefit to cover outstanding debts, burial costs, children's educational expenses, and a principal sum that can yield 75% of lost salary. (This does not include possible estate planning needs, which are covered in Chapter 10.)

In figuring a family's insurance needs, it is critical to factor in both spouses' needs, even if one does not work outside the home. Should the nonwage earner die, funds will be needed to pay for functions performed by that spouse, be it cooking, child care, or part-time assistance in a family-owned business. In all cases, your primary concern is to have adequate insurance to maintain the lifestyle to which the surviving family members are accustomed.

Exhibit 3-1 illustrates how to calculate a couple's life insurance needs.

2. *"What type of insurance policy is best for me?"* Calculating your coverage needs is only the first part of the insurance puzzle. Equally important is deciding what type of policy to buy. The two major categories of life insurance products are those that (a) do *not* accumulate cash values—generally known as **term coverage,** and (b) *do* build cash values.

In recent years, the trend has been toward term coverage because it provides the biggest bang (in terms of death benefit) per dollar of premiums paid. There is no investment component in this type of policy, so the money you pay goes purely to provide insurance.

Term Insurance

Subcategories of term insurance include annual renewable term, decreasing term, and level term. **Annual renewable term insurance** (ART) provides coverage for a year at a time. Although these policies can generally be renewed automatically, the premiums rise annually while the coverage level remains constant.

Because annual renewable term offers the highest possible death

Exhibit 3-1. Determination of life insurance needs.

Client Name: Dick Parker	Date:	11/9/93
Spouse Name: Jane Parker		

DETERMINE FINAL FUNDING REQUIREMENT:	(1)	$	25,000

Provision for final (medical/funeral) costs
(We recommend 1/4 of family's total annual
income, but no less than $25,000.)

DETERMINE TOTAL PERSONAL DEBT:	2)	$	136,000

Inclusive of home mortgage and other
outstanding debts

DETERMINE CHILD(REN'S) COLLEGE FUNDING REQUIREMENT:	3)	$	18,259

DETERMINE PRE-RETIREMENT FUNDING REQUIREMENT:	4)	$	56,729

Funds to support surviving spouse and/or
dependent children

YEARS UNTIL RETIREMENT: 31

Total income from both spouses:	4a)	$	75,000
(4a) × 50%	4b)	$	37,500
Less living spouse's income:	4c)	−$	35,000
TOTAL INCOME SHORTAGE:	4d)	$	2,500

DETERMINE RETIREMENT FUND REQUIREMENT:	5)	$	293,902

Funds to support surviving spouse during
retirement

YEARS UNTIL RETIREMENT: 31

Total income from both spouses:	5a)	$	75,000
TOTAL INCOME SHORTAGE: {(5a) × 50%}	5b)	$	37,500

TOTAL LIFE INSURANCE COVERAGE REQUIRED: (Add lines 1-5)	6)	$	529,890

benefit for the lowest premium, it is recommended for younger people or for those who only need life insurance for spans of less than five years.

Decreasing term insurance is just the opposite of annual renewable term, in that the premium remains constant but the death benefit declines annually. These policies are best suited for situations where the insurance need also decreases on an annual basis. For example, the policies can be ideal for mortgage cancellation coverage, whereby a home mortgage is paid off when an insured dies, relieving the surviving family members of making continued payments.

With **level term insurance,** both the premium and the death benefit remain constant for the duration of the contract, which generally covers a period of 5, 10, 15, or 20 years. In the early years of a level term policy, the premiums are generally higher than for an equal amount of annual renewable term (ART), but this flip-flops in the later years of the contract, when level term coverage becomes cheaper.

Level term contracts are recommended for those who desire to pay the lowest possible premium but require coverage for longer periods than the one- to five-year recommended time frame for ART. The best candidates for level term are generally people between the ages of 35 and 50, at the peak of their earning power.

As we have noted, term life generally provides the most coverage for the lowest price. On the negative side, however, term coverage fails to build cash values, and premiums generally rise as the contract is renewed over the years.

Whole and Universal Life

The second major category of life insurance contracts comprises those that combine insurance with a mechanism for building cash values.

Whole life insurance policies offer the stability of having premiums and death benefits that remain unchanged during the life of the policy owner. In addition, the investment component of the policy provides for a guaranteed minimum return as long as the insurance contract remains in force. Over the years, the part of your premiums set aside for investment—the money that makes up your "cash value account"—grows to a preset level.

The features found in whole life policies make them comforting to conservative individuals who prefer to have fixed coverage and costs and who favor the idea of having the insurance carrier assume the risk of investment, even if this will mean a more moderate return on their money.

But where some people gravitate toward the stability and the guarantees that are characteristic of whole life, others prefer a more flexible approach to their insurance needs. This is where **universal life insurance** comes into play. These increasingly popular contracts provide for flexible premiums and death benefits and require that the owner bear some of the risk of cash value accumulation.

To best understand the concept of universal life, think of it as a hybrid between term and whole life insurance. Under this arrangement, premium payments are first deposited into a cash value account that earns a competitive rate of return. From this account, the carrier deducts the cost of insurance (the "term" cost) as well as agent commissions and administrative expenses.

The flexibility factor built into universal life stems from the policy owner's ability to vary the premium payments and to change the death benefit in accordance with evolving financial needs. When it comes to premiums, the owner has sufficient latitude to skip payments from time to time (providing there is sufficient cash value in the policy to cover the term insurance and other costs) and to deposit more money than required in order to build cash values.

On the downside, in the event that the cash value within a universal life policy falls below projections and is thus inadequate to cover the insurance costs at the current premium rate, the owner will be required to deposit more money into the policy or the coverage will lapse. Unlike whole life, universal life places the investment risk in the contract with the policy owner. The trade-off in accepting more risk is a substantial reduction in premiums (as compared to whole life).

Universal life is generally recommended for those individuals with permanent insurance needs who prefer to control premium payments and cash values.

Variable life insurance takes the concept of combining investments and insurance coverage a step further. This is a hybrid of life insurance and mutual funds.

Inside a variable life contract is a pure insurance component plus an investment account that can be directed into any of a series of managed accounts similar to mutual funds. Variable life can be packaged as whole life or universal life. When you purchase a *variable whole life* policy, premiums are payable for the life of the policy, and in turn, the insurance company guarantees a minimum death benefit. Cash values, however, vary with the performance of the managed accounts in the policy's investment component.

In the case of *variable universal life*, premiums are flexible and based on the policy owner's ability to pay as well as on the performance of the investment account. Should the managed accounts perform exceptionally well, there may be sufficient funds in the investment account to pay for the insurance coverage without the owner having to pay additional premiums. Conversely, poor performance of the managed accounts may require the policy owner to pay larger premiums or face a decrease in the death benefit.

Variable life is a vehicle for combining an insurance strategy with an investment strategy. Although managed accounts are most often selected for the investment portion of the policy, many contracts will allow you to diversify your assets among various types of funds—including those invested in stocks, bonds, and money market funds. An attractive feature of this arrangement is that you can transfer investments inside the variable life policy from one fund to another without triggering income tax liabilities, even if you have earned substantial profits before making the switch.

Because investments play such a prominent role in variable life coverage, these policies should be limited to those individuals willing to accept risk in return for the potential to maximize the cash value accumulation in an insurance contract. The best candidates for this coverage are individuals between the ages of 25 and 45 who have a working knowledge of mutual fund investments.

Adjustable and Single-Premium Policies

For those who are uncertain as to the type of insurance coverage they want or need at any given time in their lives, **adjustable life insurance** may fit the bill. This extremely flexible form of coverage enables policy owners to switch from term to whole life and back again as their needs change and evolve. Also on the flexibility theme, you can—within limits—raise or lower the policy's face amount, increase or decrease the premium, and lengthen or reduce the protection period.

Adjustable life is recommended for individuals whose insurance needs fluctuate (or are likely to do so) based on changing personal circumstances. For example, a salaried employee who leaves a job to start a business of his own may have increased insurance needs; however, these needs may change with fluctuating cash flows and profits from the business.

If the idea of prefunding your life insurance needs with a single premium paid at the outset of the coverage is appealing to you, **single-premium whole life insurance** is worth exploring.

Consider this another investment/insurance hybrid, with a strong emphasis on the investment component. Generally, single premium life contracts will provide you with a competitive interest rate and a death benefit of from 1.5 to 4 times the lump sum premium. Because the principal and the interest rate are guaranteed by the insurance company, you can make a quick comparison between the yields on a single-premium life policy and a bank certificate of deposit. When making the yield comparison, however, bear in mind that the insurance contract has dual advantages over the CD in that it provides a tax-free death benefit and tax-deferred income.

✳ After calculating your life insurance needs, check off Life Insurance on the Taxpayer Profile if you are underinsured or need to review your current insurance coverage.

Disability Insurance

We have addressed the role of life insurance in protecting your dependents. Let's now turn our attention to another important defensive strategy: the purchase of disability protection.

Unfortunately, many people overlook disability insurance or underestimate its significance. This can be a dangerous miscalculation. Although most responsible individuals recognize the importance of insuring their homes, cars, and other valuable assets, all too many fail to protect the income stream that allows them to pay for these assets.

With this in mind, ask yourself this difficult question: "What would happen if illness or injury prevented me from engaging in my occupation and therefore cut off my salary or other income?" The answer, as hard as it may be to accept, is that it could wipe out your family's life savings and investments and could ultimately leave you destitute.

If you think disability is a remote likelihood that plagues only an unfortunate few, think again: Statistics reveal that one out of every three individuals will suffer a long-term disability (extending an average of five years) prior to retirement.

In fact, before age 65, the chances of suffering a disability that lasts three months or longer are greater than the chance of dying (by the following ratios):

At age 35:	1.63 to 1
" " 45:	1.27 to 1
" " 55:	1.71 to 1

The average duration of a disability prior to age 65 is:

At age 35: 2.9 years
" " *45:* 3.4 years
" " *55:* 2.9 years

Our goal here is not to frighten you but to help you shake the complacency that may have prevented you from purchasing disability insurance in the past. The benefits from these policies will provide the funds for you and your family to pay the costs of food, clothing, mortgage, and other daily living expenses that will continue even if you are no longer able to collect an income.

When you make the choice to buy disability coverage, keep in mind that benefits are paid after a so-called elimination period that generally extends from 30 to 90 days after you are disabled. Opting for a 90-day elimination period, as opposed to 30 days, can reduce disability premiums 15–20%.

Once benefits are paid, they generally last until the period of disability is over, or the insured reaches the age of 65. But because certain policies pay for shorter periods, such as five years, it is critical to determine the payment term when comparing one policy to another and before deciding on the purchase of a particular disability contract.

The amount of disability insurance available to you is based on a percentage of your monthly income. Although this percentage varies by carrier, many insurance companies cap the maximum coverage at 70% of salary.

How do you figure your disability coverage needs? The best approach is to calculate your monthly take-home pay, total the sources of income that would replace your paycheck were you unable to work, and compute the gap between what you are getting and what you would need.

Assume, for example, that your monthly income is $3,000. Were you disabled, you might discover that you were entitled to $350 a month in Social Security payments and $1,000 from an employer-sponsored group disability plan, for a total monthly benefit of $1,350. Disability carriers will insure you to 70% (or $2,100) of your income.

Here is how to compute the income gap that you will need to fill with disability insurance.

Current monthly take-home pay: $3,000
Less existing disability benefits:

Social Security	350
Employer-sponsored group disability plan	1,000
Total existing benefits:	$1,350
Monthly disability benefits needed to maintain current income level:	$1,650

If you have substantial investment assets in a personal account, you may want to consider using the income generated by those assets to fill a part of the gap between your paycheck and your disability coverage. Rather than reinvest the portfolio income and dividends, take a percentage of them as distributions in order to maintain your standard of living while you are out of work.

Also bear in mind that if you have funds in a qualified plan, you may be able to withdraw income from the plan (without paying the standard penalty for premature distributions) during your disability. Both of these options can be used to minimize your insurance needs or to supplement insurance coverage beyond the 70% limitation.

But don't think of this approach as a substitute for insurance: Withdrawing the earnings from an investment portfolio over an extended period of time may prevent the portfolio from keeping pace with inflation. Additionally, using retirement savings prematurely will jeopardize your ability to retire with financial independence.

Additional Facts About Disability Insurance

* Premium rates are based on the amount of coverage, the term of coverage, and the term of the elimination period. Individuals capable of sustaining the first 90 days of disability without insurance assistance (a position you can reach by using this book's approach to money management) can take advantage of the most attractive premiums.
* Policy renewable features vary by company. The best coverage is a "guaranteed, non-cancellable policy" in which the client can maintain coverage (generally until age 65) and premiums never increase.
* Monthly disability benefits are generally received income-tax free.

Warning: Before agreeing to a particular disability policy, you should always heed these two precautions:

1. Make certain that you are entitled to full coverage if you are unable to perform the duties and obligations of *your* occupation as opposed

to any occupation. Without this clause, the carrier could refuse to pay benefits to a surgeon earning $150,000 a year who cannot perform surgery but who can work for $50,000 a year as a medical aide.

2. Look for policies that pay if you are only partially disabled and are capable of earning part of your ordinary income. In this case, you will want coverage that makes up the gap in lost income. Make certain the policy does not require that you first be fully disabled before collecting this partial benefit, as you may never have a complete disability.

❋ Check off Disability Insurance on the Taxpayer Profile if you need to have your disability insurance needs reviewed.

Health Insurance

With many employers reducing and even eliminating company-paid health insurance, and federal health care reform an uncertain proposition, individuals unaccustomed to paying for this increasingly costly coverage may soon have to foot part or all of the bill. Unfortunately, there are no simple solutions for absorbing this cost in your budget. But there are some ways to trim premiums to make them somewhat more affordable:

* If your employer no longer offers attractive coverage terms, check with groups, clubs, or professional organizations you belong to. See if they offer group coverage and if their plans are more affordable than your company's policies.
* If you can afford to absorb part of the cost of routine medical treatment, elect policy deductibles higher than standard. Generally, the higher the deductible, the lower the premiums.
* Again, if you can pay for part of the cost of medical care, select a higher co-insurance ratio (the part of the bill you pay). This will also bring down premiums with many types of coverage.

❋ Check off Health Insurance on the Taxpayer Profile if you need to have your health insurance needs reviewed.

Property and Casualty Insurance

A comprehensive insurance portfolio, of course, calls for property and casualty policies to protect against the loss of your home and car.

When securing homeowners coverage, look for policies that provide for automatic replacement cost of your home. This means that regardless of how much the property appreciates, the coverage will be sufficient to rebuild your home in the event of fire or other covered catastrophes.

Also be sure to obtain "floaters" in the policy to protect against the loss of itemized valuables such as jewelry, furs, and collectibles. *Electing a high deductible can substantially lower your premiums on both home and auto insurance policies.*

Personal umbrella liability policies provide extra protection beyond the limits of your homeowners and auto insurance. Considering that jury awards in liability cases can reach enormous sums, umbrella policies can provide an invaluable buffer of protection for modest premiums. Figure $150 annually for the first $1 million in coverage; less for each $1 million increment.

---

* Check off Property and Casualty Insurance on the Taxpayer Profile if you need to have your home or auto insurance needs reviewed.

Paying for College

If you have children—even preschoolers—the number you write on the exemptions line should remind you of yet another need: to provide your children with a college education.

A U.S. Census Bureau report emphasizes the strong correlation between a college education and higher earnings. According to the report, college graduates outearn those with high school diplomas by more than $360,000 over the course of a normal working lifetime. Clearly, a college education is an investment that pays off.

But first you must accumulate the funds for that investment. Considering the soaring costs of room, board, and tuition—and the huge bite this can take out of a family's income—the smartest way to pay for college is to begin investing for it well before your children reach the age of 18. This way, the power of compounding can work for you over the years.

Dollar Cost Averaging

One effective approach is to make monthly contributions to an educational fund that you establish with a series of mutual funds. Every time you make a payment to a fund, you receive a confirmation and a return envelope for additional investments. Treat this as a monthly bill—just as important as your auto loan and your telephone charges—and pay it without fail.

This provides the discipline to fund an account that builds substantially over the years. Furthermore, because you are setting aside the same amount each month, you will benefit from an investment strategy known as "dollar cost averaging." This means that should the value of your mutual funds drop from time to time, your investment enables you to acquire more shares per dollar. As the funds appreciate over the long term, you will have an ever greater number of shares and ultimately (should your funds perform well) substantial gains on your investments.

The question is, how much will you have to save on a monthly basis to provide sufficient funds to finance your children's education? Naturally, this depends on the type of school the children attend (private, elite private, or public college), the number of years you have to save, and the prevailing inflation rate over those years.

All of these variables must be factored in to arrive at a precise number. But you can calculate a rough estimate of the monthly savings required for each child to attend a public college (figuring $46,000 for a four-year education) by dividing $4,000 by the number of years remaining before the child reaches 21. For example, for an eleven-year-old child, you would have to save $400 per month in order to accumulate the necessary funds. This assumes that your investments can achieve a return equal to the rate of inflation (see Exhibit 3-2).

The Trust Fund

When saving money for education, it may be wise to do so through a so-called Uniform Gift to Minors Act (UGMA) account. With this approach, the funds are placed in a trust for the benefit of a child. In this way, funds accumulating in the trust are taxed at the minor's tax rate rather than the parents' higher rate. (This tax break is limited, however, to $1,200 of income for children under 14 years of age; income in excess of $1,200 in any given year is taxed at the parents' rate—the so-called kiddy tax.)

The downside to a UGMA is that the child receives all the assets at

Exhibit 3-2. How much to invest now to pay future college costs.

College Timer				
	To Accumulate			
	25,000	50,000	75,000	100,000
Age*	Set Aside $/Month			
1	52	104	157	209
2	58	117	175	235
3	66	132	198	264
4	74	149	224	299
5	85	170	255	340
6	97	194	291	388
7	111	223	334	446
8	129	258	388	517
9	151	302	453	604
10	178	358	536	715
11	214	429	644	859
12	263	526	789	1,053
13	331	663	994	1,326
14	435	869	1,304	1,739
15	607	1,215	1,822	2,430
16	955	1,909	2,864	3,818
17	1,999	3,998	5,996	7,995

Based on annual rate of return of 9% rounded to the nearest dollar.
*At inception of program.

age 18 and can literally do anything with the funds—whether or not you, the parent, approve of her choices.

But there are other kinds of trusts that give you not only a tax break, but also a measure of control over how the trust money will be used. For example: If you own an asset that has appreciated in value over the years, and the asset is sold, you will be subject to a substantial tax on the gain. To avoid this, you may want to set up a **charitable remainder trust.**

It works this way: By contributing the asset to the trust, you not only avoid the taxation, but, as a sweetener, you receive a charitable deduction that can be used to offset certain taxable income. The trust can be structured so that the asset can be sold with the proceeds placed in investments that generate income. This income is then paid to the child, in accordance with the trust documents, and can be used for educational purposes. With this goal in mind, you may stipulate that the child (as the beneficiary of the trust) be paid a fixed amount of money over four years, beginning the year the child reaches 18 years of age. (Have an attorney structure the trust for you as well as advise you of the relevant rules, caveats, and limitations.)

Beating the "Kiddy Tax"

As we just mentioned, when you invest for children under 14 years of age, all investment income over $1,200 is taxed at the parents' rate. This means the income and dividends earned will be lumped together with the parents' earnings, thus increasing your taxes and reducing the amount of money available for continued investment.

Fortunately, there are ways to counter this kiddy tax. One approach is to place some or all of the children's investments in tax-exempt or tax-deferred vehicles. In this way, earnings on the investments do not add to your tax obligation.

If you like the sound of this, your best options include tax-free mutual funds and unit investment trusts, discussed in Chapter 2. These provide an effective means of legally detouring the kiddy tax.

Your Time Frame

Just how long you have to save for college is a major determinant of the appropriate investment vehicles for building your education fund. In general, if you have three years or less, limit your investments to stable, conservative vehicles. Although the yields will be modest, capital—which you will need shortly—will be preserved.

A time frame of five years provides a bit more leeway, enabling you to trade up in yield with minor risk of capital fluctuation.

Should you have the luxury of more than five years to build your education fund, you have a wide range of options. Because the money is not needed for a substantial period, you can afford to make relatively aggressive investments, confident that you have the time to ride out the market cycles. This provides the greatest opportunity for substantial capital appreciation and is another reason why a college accumulation fund should be started even before a child enters kindergarten.

When you have more than five years and thus the opportunity to accept some risk in return for the prospect of higher returns, use a diversified approach to hedge your risks. Although the government and other income instruments in the portfolio may reduce the overall return (as compared to an investment in growth stock funds alone), these more conservative investments provide balance and downside protection against substantial capital loss during economic downturns. This is especially

Investment Options by Time Frame

	Years Until College		
	Under 3 Years	3–5 Years	5+ Years
Recommended type of investment	* Money market fund * Short-term bond fund * CDs	U.S. government securities funds	* *Defensive:* U.S. government securities funds * *Moderate:* Growth and income funds * *Aggressive:* Growth equity funds

important if the fund must be invaded before college in order to provide for personal emergencies.

In Case of Emergency

To limit the financial damage caused by one type of personal emergency, you may wish to add an educational funding rider to your disability insurance. When available from your insurance carrier, this allows you to accumulate a deferred monthly disability benefit that can be used for college expenses. For each month you are disabled, a proportionate benefit is accrued, to be paid in a lump sum when the covered child reaches 18. If you are still disabled at that time, and the entire benefit has not accrued, you may receive the accrued lump sum, plus a monthly benefit until the maximum benefit amount is reached.

Example: Gordon, a dentist, purchases a $40,000 educational funding rider for his daughter. He becomes disabled at age 42 (when his daughter is 13 years old) and remains disabled for 4 years. Following the one-year elimination period, the educational rider begins to accrue $670 per month. Because Gordon remains disabled for 36 more months, a benefit of nearly $25,000 accrues, which will be paid in a lump sum when Gordon's daughter reaches 18, whether or not he is disabled. If he remains disabled after her 18th birthday, he will have received the lump sum, plus the monthly accrual until the $40,000 maximum is reached.

＊ Check off Education Funds on the Taxpayer Profile if you have children for whom you would like to establish an education fund.

Your Will

One final issue to think about when filling out Line 6 of your 1040: If you have dependents of any kind, creating or updating a will is imperative. That's because a will:

* Can make provisions for family income immediately after the death of the major breadwinner. This is done by allowing the executor of the estate to release funds or assets to the beneficiaries.
* Designates a trusted individual to handle the affairs of your estate, principally protecting the assets for the benefit of family members.
* Provides for the explicit transfer of tangible personal property not held in joint tenancy.
* Provides a trust mechanism for the benefit of children (especially important in cases where both parents die).

Although you may have always considered wills to be permanent documents, they must be reviewed for updating (to reflect a changing legal environment) every five years, or sooner if a major new inheritance-related law is passed. Other factors mandating a review include movement of your principal residence from one state to another, a change in family status (such as a divorce or the birth of a child), or increases or decreases in your debt or income levels.

For a detailed discussion of estate planning, see Chapter 10.

＊ Check off Develop/Review Will on the Taxpayer Profile.

Chapter 4

Sources of Income—A Road Map to Investment Options: Line 7

> The people who get on in this world are the people who get up and look for the circumstances they want, and, if they can't find them, make them.
>
> George Bernard Shaw

Many of us worry a great deal about the amount of income we earn, but few stop to consider the sources of that income and their relevance to the creation of a successful long-term financial plan. That may be a costly oversight—one that a review of your tax return can help to correct.

By taking a close look at each component of the "wages, salaries, and tips" reported on Form 1040, Line 7—for the source of the income as well as the sum—you learn about the retirement, deferred compensation, and pension plans in which you are eligible to participate.

The Right Income Source

This is critical because the right income source—the right job, with the right benefits—can allow you to contribute, on a tax-advantaged basis, to 401(k), defined benefit, defined contribution, and nonqualified deferred compensation plans, all of which are discussed in this chapter. These plans can be vital for accumulating wealth and achieving financial freedom.

Now, let's explore the retirement plans that are provided most often through your place of business (SEPs and Keogh plans will be discussed in Chapter 6; IRAs, in Chapter 7. For a comparison of various plans, see Appendix B, the H. D. Vest Retirement Plan Guide).

power of consistent saving and investing, and once you develop the discipline to invest even a modest portion of your income, all of these rewards can be yours.

Once again, your tax return can help in this process. If you add up the gross income reported on your Form 1040 over a period of years, you will likely be surprised just how much money you earn over time and in turn how great a pool of money there is to work with.

The fact is, most people—even those who consider themselves ordinary, middle-class workers—earn a fortune during their lifetime. Yes, a fortune. The proof, and a startling proof it can be, is in the numbers. Assume, for example, that your career spans ages 25 to 65 and during that time your income remains fixed at a modest $20,000 a year. You may think you've scraped by, but the fact is you have earned $800,000 over the course of your lifetime.

Increase the hypothetical salary figure to $30,000 a year and your career earnings soar to more than $1 million. Add in a factor for regular wage increases over the years (which is clearly the norm) and you have a picture of a "middle-income" worker producing $2 million or more over a lifetime. And you say you don't have enough to save and invest even small sums on a regular basis? The figures prove you wrong.

All we suggest is that you defer a portion of your monthly earnings from current spending and direct it toward investing for wealth creation and the ability to finance future needs. The failure to do so has dramatic, and potentially disastrous, implications.

EXAMPLE: Carol Foley worked from age 25 to age 65, starting at $25,000 and with a $1,000 raise each year, ending at $65,000. By the time Carol retired, she had generated total earnings of nearly $2 million ($1,845,000 to be more precise). Now assuming she spent all of her earnings as they were made, relying solely on her company's pension plan and Social Security to carry her through retirement, Carol's standard of living fell to 60% of its previous level, if not lower (see Exhibit 4-1).

Again, the critical lesson is that it's not what you earn that counts, but what you keep. If you spend all of your earnings during your working years, when your earnings stop, your standard of living will fall dramatically. You will, as the saying goes, have to pay the piper.

Now let's look at another, more favorable scenario, an intelligent plan that takes into account current as well as future needs.

EXAMPLE: Jane Wagner took a long-term view of her goals and, at 25, decided to begin investing 10% of her income. Although, at first blush, it might seem that investing relatively small sums would produce

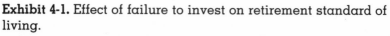

Exhibit 4-1. Effect of failure to invest on retirement standard of living.

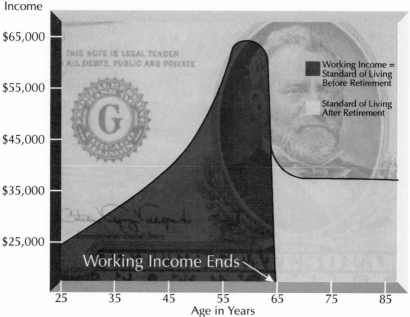

meager returns, once again the numbers indicate just the opposite. By investing 10% of $1,845,000 earned during her working years, Jane produced an additional $1,648,629 from investment earnings by age 65 (assuming an annual 10% compounded rate of return).

Jane's standard of living between the ages of 25 and 65 was hardly affected by a 10% decrease in disposable income. Certainly, she had to exercise some self-discipline; perhaps forgoing a number of clothing accessories, or purchasing a lesser-model car or one with fewer options. Still, the overall impact on Jane's lifestyle was minimal (see Exhibit 4-2).

In the retirement years, the benefit of making these minimal sacrifices proves enormous. In Jane's case, we can figure about $184,000 of investment dollars from income savings (10% of her $1,845,000 career earnings) plus investment interest and dividends of $1,648,629. Factoring in assumed pension and Social Security payments of approximately $39,000 a year, and the yield from her retirement nest egg, Jane stands to collect an income of $222,262 a year, thus tremendously enhancing her post-retirement standard of living.

Exhibit 4-2. Standard of living after retirement for an individual
saving 10% of income during working life.

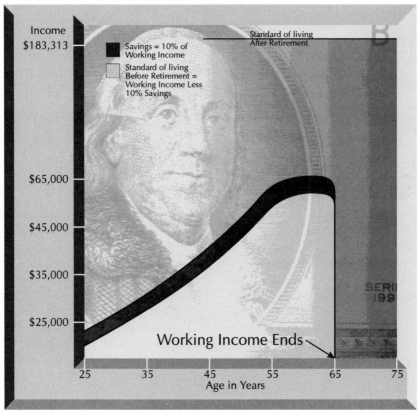

Income	
$183,313	■ Savings = 10% of Working Income
	☐ Standard of living Before Retirement = Working Income Less 10% Savings

Standard of living
After Retirement

$65,000

$45,000

$35,000

$25,000

Working Income Ends

25   35   45   55   65   75
Age in Years

Note: Assumes 10% annual rate or return compounded at the beginning of the year.

Although consistent investing appears to perform magic with your
personal finances, there is nothing mysterious at work here. No smoke.
No mirrors. No sleight of hand. It is simply the combined power of discipline (to save as well as spend) and compounding.

But there is a caveat here—one we have mentioned before but that
bears repetition. That is, the power of compounding and, in turn, of
wealth creation works best the earlier in life you begin. Saving $100 a
month beginning at age 30 produces a $379,664 portfolio by age 65 (as-
suming a 10% yield compounded monthly). Wait until 40 to begin the

same $100 a month savings plan, and the retirement nest egg shrinks to $132,683; begin at age 50 and it shrivels to $41,447.

Don't get us wrong: It is never too late (just as it is never too early) to begin an investment program. But the longer you wait, one of two things will happen: (1) You will have to invest more monthly or annually to achieve the same lump sum at retirement; (2) Lacking the extra money to catch up, you will wind up with significantly less money at retirement.

Here is another illustration of the power of time.

EXAMPLE: James Reed has a long-term perspective as a young working man and starts an IRA at age 23. He invests $2,000 annually for 5 years (for a total of $10,000) and then, due to conditions beyond his control, he stops making IRA contributions. Even so, if the money is allowed to accumulate over the years at a 12% rate of return, he will have $1,055,576 at retirement.

However, if Reed's friend Michael Mazur waits only 5 more years to open his IRA, in this case at age 28, he would have to invest $2,000 annually for 36 years in order to have a million dollars by age 65. Comparing Reed and Mazur, we could say that in the goal of amassing $1 million at retirement, the former did it the easy way (using time to his advantage) and the latter did it the hard way.

Although we have seen quite clearly that time is a critical factor in wealth creation, we must also reemphasize the importance of return. The all-important risk-reward ratio is not an intellectual exercise. As you view the various investment options at your disposal—including blue-chip stocks, aggressive growth stocks, high-rated bonds, low-rated bonds, government obligations, and money market funds—you must keep in mind that trading some measure of security in exchange for a potentially higher rate of return can have a powerful impact on your wealth creation.

For example, a difference of just four percentage points on a $100 monthly investment program can produce a portfolio that is more than twice as big over 30 years. Nothing can speak more powerfully of the importance of adding some element of prudent risk to your investment portfolio.

The Rule of 72

To evaluate the impact of various investment options on your wealth-building program, you can make a rapid calculation by using the so-called Rule of 72. This indicates how quickly your money will double at a given rate of return. To make the calculation, divide the number 72 by the rate of return. For example, $10,000 invested at 10% will double to $20,000 in 7.2 years; but at 12% it will double in just six years (Exhibit 4-3).

Questions and Answers

By this point, we have showered you with a great deal of information about financial planning and wealth building, all with the aim of providing you with the right habits and the investment options to achieve financial security.

Much of this information may be new to you. If so, you surely have

Exhibit 4-3. How to compute the Rule of 72.

72	÷	Rate of Return	=	Years to Double Your Dollars
		24%		3
		18%		4
		12%		6
		10%		7.2
		6%		12
		4%		18

questions about our concepts of risk and reward, investment strategies, and diversification. Let's address some of your probable concerns head on:

Q: *You are telling me to invest in equities and other securities that bear some risk, but I am concerned that these investments will suffer in the event of inflation, recession, or worldwide political instability. Don't I have a legitimate right to be concerned?*

A: Of course you have a right to be concerned—but you should not let fear stop you from making intelligent, long-term decisions. There will always be economic volatility; the fact remains, however, that people with discipline and foresight make substantial sums of money in periods of short-term crisis.

People talk all the time about "buying low and selling high," but doing so consistently is nothing more than a pipe dream. The best approach is to buy quality and to buy it consistently, using dollar cost averaging (see the section earlier in this chapter under "Paying for College") to smooth out the price cycles. The only "right time" to start an investment program is now. As we have shown you, the earlier you begin, the more dramatic your results are likely to be.

Q. *I keep adding up my income and my expenses and the numbers tell me I cannot afford to start an investment program. What do I do?*

A. Start by recognizing that you can't afford *not* to start an investment program. When you go over your budget, make a provision to pay yourself first. That has to be your first priority. Savings for education or retirement cannot be done with money left over. Instead, they must be paid for like any other bill, every month. Over time, this disciplined approach will produce substantial sums, as we have illustrated.

Once you get in the habit of investing a modest portion of your earnings on a regular basis, you will not miss the money you are directing to your future and you will be on your way toward financial independence.

Q. *Why can't I put all of my money in FDIC-insured certificates of deposit and avoid all risk? Doesn't that make more sense than subjecting myself to the uncertainties of the financial markets?*

A. As we have noted, a concern over safety is entirely appropriate. But you cannot let it paralyze you or severely limit your investment options to the point that you have no chance of building a portfolio that outpaces inflation.

The fact is, CDs are inappropriate investment vehicles for long-term savings and retirement programs. With their relatively modest yields and the impact of taxation, your investment in CDs may actually lose purchasing power over time. We are not suggesting that you be reckless with your money—that violates our approach—but we do maintain that some risk must be accepted to achieve satisfactory returns over time (see the discussion of the Bennetts and the Sorensens in Chapter 1).

Q. *You seem to place a great deal of emphasis on mutual funds. Why should I invest this way rather than in specific stocks and bonds that appear attractive to me?*

A. Let us begin to answer your question by asking another question. If we were to give you $100,000 today and tell you that you could either allocate all of the money to a single stock (one you had a hunch would do well) or you could invest the money into several different vehicles, which option would you choose?

When you think about it, you will probably prefer to spread out your investment over a variety of securities to protect your capital should your hunch prove wrong. That's simply good, common sense. As we have seen, spreading investments over several vehicles reduces risk. If you put the entire $100,000 into the hunch stock and that investment declines in value, you could lose big—perhaps the entire sum.

On the other hand, if you balance your portfolio by diversifying in several investment options, even if some of the investments decline in value, the increases in others will likely compensate for this, perhaps boosting the value of the total portfolio.

This is precisely how mutual funds work and why we favor them as investment vehicles for a substantial portion of your portfolio. With mutuals, you have the best of both worlds: diversification plus the benefit of experienced professionals who monitor the markets and manage your money on an active basis. Few of us can match that kind of safety and performance by investing on our own.

Nonqualified Deferred Compensation

Let's return to Line 7 of Form 1040—wages, salaries, and tips—and consider the benefits of a form of payment known as nonqualified deferred compensation.

Simply put, this means that you arrange to have a portion of the income currently due you paid in subsequent years. Naturally, this is not for everyone. First, you need the clout to structure such an arrangement with your employer (which means you are likely to be a relatively highly paid executive). Second, you need the financial flexibility and wherewithal to forgo accepting all current income in the year it is earned.

If you can qualify for deferred compensation, these appealing benefits will be available to you:

Benefits of Deferred Compensation Plans

+ You can reduce your current tax obligation by shifting income to subsequent years.

+ You can invest the deferred earnings for retirement, children's education, or other long-term financial objectives. Deferring and investing income in this way provides a tax-advantaged mechanism for the systematic savings you need to achieve financial independence.

+ The deferred income can also be set aside as a fund to provide for your family in the event of your death or disability.

Deferred compensation plans are structured as "funded" and "unfunded." A **funded deferred compensation plan** identifies specific assets the employer allocates to pay the deferred compensation. For the plan to qualify as funded, the employee must have a current beneficial interest in the assets.

An **unfunded deferred compensation plan,** by contrast, is based on an unsecured promise to pay the future benefit. Although the employer may have a strategy for accumulating the cash necessary to pay the benefits, no assets (in which the employee has a current interest) are specifically earmarked for this purpose.

Clearly, as an employee, you may prefer a funded deferred compensation plan precisely because it guarantees that the benefit will be paid. Your present beneficial interest in the assets funding the plan removes them from the reach of the employer's general creditors.

But in gauging the relative merits of funded and unfunded plans, there is more to consider than the degree of assurance that the deferred benefit will be paid. For example, if your goal is to avoid taxation until the benefit is actually *received* (rather than being taxed at the time the benefit is simply granted), the unfunded plan is preferable. The ability to defer taxation in this way is the major appeal of the unfunded option.

Typically, deferred compensation is available in one or more of these three formats: executive bonus plans, salary continuation plans, and salary reduction SEPs.

Executive Bonus Plans

Executive bonus plans are generally funded with a dividend-paying whole life insurance policy. Typically, the employer obtains the insurance coverage on the executive and then pays the premium directly to the insurance company. As the policy builds cash value over the years (a key feature of whole life coverage), the executive's wealth increases in tandem. An attractive feature is that the executive's interest in the policy compounds on a tax-deferred basis, thus putting more money to work to achieve financial objectives.

Under the terms of so-called 162(a) executive bonus plans, the employer is entitled to deduct the amount of the whole life premiums paid on your behalf. Although you have to declare the premiums as additional income, and, in turn, pay the tax on this sum, you can use your policy dividends to offset all or part of this liability.

Additional Benefits of Executive Bonus Plans

+ As the employee, you own all rights to the insurance policy.
+ If the employer-paid policy replaces a preexisting policy, your out-of-pocket costs are reduced, often substantially.
+ In the event that you change employers, the insurance policy—with its cash accumulation—can be taken with you. (Of course, the new employer may not choose to continue paying the premiums.)
+ Your beneficiaries pay no income tax on the death benefit.

If you like the idea of an executive bonus plan and need ammunition to convince your employer to make the program available to you, try informing management that the company stands to gain these benefits:

* The costs of the plan are tax-deductible to the company when the employee recognizes the benefit as income.
* The plans are 100% discriminatory, meaning they can be offered to small groups of employees without being offered to others in the company. Who gets what is left to management's discretion.
* IRS approval is not required to launch a plan.
* The company can set the amount of its contributions (premium payments) at management's discretion. There are no minimums or maximums.
* The plans are relatively simple to structure and administer.
* The plans can be terminated at any time.

Salary Continuation Plans

With a salary continuation plan, an employer agrees to make contributions or to provide a benefit in addition to the employee's current compensation. This plan is also referred to as a supplemental income plan. It is appropriate under the following conditions:

* The employee has not reached the limits of reasonable compensation.
* The employer can afford and is willing to pay the added cost above the employee's salary.
* The employer wants to apply "golden handcuffs" to a valued employee—that is, an inducement to remain with the employer for the long term.

Salary-Reduction SEPs

SEP stands for Simplified Employee Pension, a type of retirement plan favored by many small businesses. One kind of Simplified Employee Pension plan, known as the SAR-SEP or salary-reduction SEP, allows you to defer compensation.

Employers considering the establishment of salary-reduction SEPs must meet the following tests:

* The company must have fewer than 25 employees eligible to join the plan.
* Contributions of the highest-paid employees cannot exceed 1.25 times the average contribution of those at the low end of the salary spectrum. Other tests must also be met to prevent the plan from discriminating against lower-paid employees.
* A minimum of 50% of eligible employees must participate in the salary deferral component of the plan.

SEPs are discussed in greater detail in Chapter 6.

---

* Return to Line 7 of the Taxpayer Profile and check the applicable retirement and insurance plans that are available to you through your employer. Make sure you are participating fully in these programs.

Chapter 5

A Snapshot of Your Personal Finances— Interest, Dividends, Diversification, and Annuities: Lines 8a, 8b, and 9

> Success is a journey, not a destination.
>
> Ben Sweetland

Now we come to a critical segment of your tax return, Lines 8a, 8b, and 9, where you must report taxable interest and dividend income earned during the year. If your earnings in either category exceed $400, you must file a Schedule B form detailing the stocks, bonds, mutual funds, savings accounts, certificates of deposit, and other investment vehicles that produced the income.

The Schedule B Snapshot

Upon first inspection, Schedule B appears to be little more than an inventory of your investments provided for tax compliance purposes. But as you move to maximize wealth creation and achieve financial independence, look at Schedule B as a snapshot of your personal finances—one that leads you to ask critical questions:

* Am I properly diversified?
* What type of return am I receiving on my investments?
* Am I in a high tax bracket, and do my investments reflect this?
* If so, have I considered ways to exempt some of my earnings from taxes, such as retirement plans, annuities, and other tax-exempt or tax-deferred vehicles?

Let's explore a number of the key issues one at a time.

Diversification

If your Schedule B inventory reveals that the bulk of your interest and dividends is generated by a small number of stocks and bonds, chances are you are doing yourself a disservice.

Why?

First, investing in individual securities—and doing it profitably— demands the time and experience to make appropriate selections on the basis of solid information rather than hunches or tips. You'll also need the expertise to track the securities' performance and to make the all-important judgment call on when to buy and sell. Chances are that unless you are a professional money manager, you come up short on all of these counts.

Second, the reliance on a few isolated stocks and bonds as the bedrock of your portfolio means you lack adequate diversification. Put another way, you have too many eggs in too few baskets.

As we have emphasized, successful investing over the intermediate to long term requires a mix of securities that gives your portfolio balance through all of the economic cycles and conditions. For example, the portfolio of a couple in their mid-40s with $50,000 to invest would likely fare well with the following components (allocated as shown in Exhibit 5-1):

Equities:	20%
Fixed-income securities:	25%
Real estate:	20%
International stocks and bonds:	20%
Precious metals:	10%
Energy:	5%

Exhibit 5-1. How to divide the investment pie.

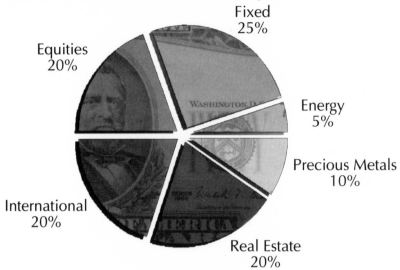

Fixed
25%

Equities
20%

Energy
5%

Precious Metals
10%

International
20%

Real Estate
20%

❋ On the Taxpayer Profile, fill in the amounts of interest and dividends from your Form 1040, Lines 8a, 8b, and 9; if 0, enter 0. If you have investments that should be reviewed for suitability and diversification, check Yes for "Existing investment portfolio" and check "Analyze portfolio and review financial objectives." If you have investments in individual stocks and bonds, check Yes for "Individual stocks and bonds" and check "Reinvest into diversified portfolio."

Rate of Return

The Schedule B inventory may well reveal that your investment approach to date is overly cautious, resulting in a paltry return that barely keeps up with inflation. This can have a devastating impact on the accumulation of capital over the years. Just look at the difference in net result between investing $100 a month at 15% as opposed to 10%.

Value of $100 Per Month Invested Over Time

Years	10%	15%	Difference
10	$ 21,037	$ 28,018	$ 6,981
20	75,602	141,372	65,770
30	217,131	599,948	382,817
40	584,222	2,455,144	1,870,922

As the numbers make abundantly clear, trading up to the higher return can produce a difference of nearly $2 million over 40 years (assuming reinvestment of interest and dividends).

If you have more than five years to invest, you would be wise to shift at least part of your investments out of CDs and money market funds and into such higher return options as equity mutual funds. This can have a powerful impact on your portfolio's rate of return.

The key point to remember is the risk–reward ratio that we have reviewed several times but that bears repeating. In order to outpace inflation and to accumulate real wealth over the years, you must accept some measure of risk.

With this in mind, let's take another look at common stocks. You may fear stocks because you know the stock market moves in cyclical patterns. There is no denying this. Historically, stock prices have demonstrated wide fluctuations.

But rather than focus on this volatility, a prudent, long-term investor will focus instead on another undeniable fact: Over the years, the market has moved upward. This is precisely why stock ownership can build wealth. In fact, the market's volatility works in favor of the long-term investor by creating the opportunity for capital appreciation. By refusing to panic when market swings occur, retaining a long-term investment horizon, and continuing to make purchases on a systematic basis, you will be accumulating shares at what should prove to be bargain prices when the market resumes its upward momentum.

A reading of your Schedule B may reveal that you have gone too far in the search for maximum yields. Your portfolio may be overloaded with high-yielding securities that get whacked down to size by your high marginal tax rate. If you fit this profile, you may wind up with a greater after-tax return by skewing a portion of your investments to tax-free options.

How can you tell if a tax-free investment will benefit you? The answer depends on the relative yields of taxable and tax-free investments and your tax rate. Assume, for example, that you plan to invest $100,000 in either a 30-year U.S. Treasury bond or a municipal bond investment vehicle with an average portfolio life of 25 to 30 years.

For the sake of comparison, we will use the average yield of 30-year Treasury bonds for February 7, 1991, and the average yield of the Bond Buyer 20 for the same date. As Exhibit 5-2 indicates, net annual income is greater with the long-term municipal bond investment, at both the 28% and 31% tax rates.

If you are interested in making a tax-free investment but are confused about the options available to you, consider the distinctive advantages of tax-free unit trusts, mutual funds, and closed-end funds as shown in Exhibit 5-3.

Look into municipal bonds issued by a single state, paying interest which is 100% free of both state and federal taxes for residents of the issuing state. In some states, interest is also free from local income taxes, making the income "triple tax-free."

Assume your combined federal and state tax rate is 39.5%. To find the taxable equivalent yield (the yield of a taxable investment equivalent

Exhibit 5-2. Tax-free income equivalent yields.

Taxable Income		Taxable Income	
Long-term Treasury Bond		*Long-term* Municipal Investment	
Yielding 8.03% per year		Yielding 6.86% per year	
28% tax rate		28% tax rate	
Invest $100,000		Invest $100,000	
Annual gross income	$8,030	Annual gross income	$6,860
Taxes	2,248	Taxes	0
Net annual income	$5,782	Net annual income	$6,860
31% tax rate		31% tax rate	
Annual gross income	$8,030	Annual gross income	$6,860
Taxes	2,489	Taxes	0
Net annual income	$5,541	Net annual income	$6,860

Investors in both the 28% and 31% tax brackets came out ahead with this tax-free municipal investment.

Over a thirty year period, the investor in the 28% tax bracket could keep an additional $32,340 from his tax-free investment.

Over the same thirty year period, the investor in the 31% tax bracket could keep an additional $39,570 from his tax-free investment.

Exhibit 5-3. Distinctive advantages of tax-free unit trusts, mutual funds, and closed-end funds.

Unit Trusts	Open-end Mutual Funds	Closed-end Funds
Key Objectives		
To assemble a portfolio which will provide a steady flow of tax-free income for the life of the trust.	To provide as high a level of tax-free income as can be achieved with ongoing management and purchase of investment grade* securities, while preserving capital.	To provide an attractive tax-free yield. Some funds also provide the opportunity for enhancement of portfolio value through the purchase of under-valued securities.
Benefits		
Steady tax-free income from a "fixed" portfolio of municipal bonds with a specific average maturity. Scheduled return of principal.	Variable tax-free income from a "flexible" portfolio of municipal bonds which is managed to take advantage of changing market conditions. Changeable average maturity.	Variable tax-free income from a closed-end managed portfolio of municipal bonds. Changeable average maturity.
Income can be used to meet periodic expenses for retirement, mortgage payments and insurance premiums.	Income can be reinvested into additional shares of the fund for dollar-cost-averaging and tax-free asset accumulation.	Income can be reinvested into additional shares of the fund for tax-free accumulation of assets. Shares traded publicly on major stock exchanges.
Structural Characteristics		
Can issue a fixed number of redeemable units at deposit, determined by the principal amount of the underlying portfolio.	Has a changing number of shares due to new purchases and redemptions.	The number of shares issued is fixed at the conclusion of the initial public offering period, except for shares issued for reinvestment of dividends.
Units are sold at the public offering price plus accrued interest. The public offering price reflects the price of the bonds in the portfolio, calculated on a per unit basis plus the sales charge.	Shares are sold at net asset value plus the sales charge. Net asset value is determined by dividing the total net assets of the fund by the number of shares outstanding.	Shares are traded publicly on the NYSE or AMEX. Shares are not redeemed by the sponsor, but traded in the open market at a price which may be above or below net asset value based upon supply and demand for the shares themselves.
Portfolio may change if bonds are called or sold for credit reasons or to meet unit holder redemptions.	Portfolio changes with bond purchases and sales and with shareholder purchases and redemptions.	Portfolio changes with bond purchases and sales.

* The funds may also invest a small portion of their assets in unrated bonds, which in the opinion of the managers, have credit characteristics equivalent to investment grade bonds. Some funds may not invest in all investment grade or insured bonds. It is important for investors to read the prospectus.

closer, we see that if these investors were in the 28% tax bracket, their after-tax rate of return was only 5.04%. Still not terrible—but wait. Because inflation in 1987 weighed in at 4.5%, the real rate of return on the CD investment (after taxes and inflation) was a paltry 0.54%. Here's where the downside really hits home. At that rate, it would take the investors 134 years to double their money in real terms.

So while there can be a place in your portfolio for fixed annuities, remain alert to the need to protect against inflation.

Other Potential Disadvantages of Fixed Annuities:

— The Internal Revenue Service places restrictions on premature distributions made before age 59½. Although many contracts allow the investor to withdraw up to 10% of the annuity's accumulated value without triggering early withdrawal penalties from the *insurance company,* this does not eliminate *IRS* penalties. With this in mind, beware that pledging an annuity contract as collateral for a loan is also considered a premature withdrawal, thus triggering the tax penalty.
— Most insurance companies will refuse to offer annuities to individuals who have reached their 80th birthday.

Exhibit 5-4 compares the costs and benefits of CDs and fixed annuities.

Variable Annuities

If a fixed annuity is similar to a CD, a variable annuity can be thought of as a mutual fund family wrapped inside an annuity contract. Where the fixed annuity offers safety and stability, the variable annuity offers flexibility and the opportunity to achieve substantially higher returns.

Variable annuities offer these key features:

* Selection of separate accounts within the annuity contract, thus allowing you to diversify your assets among a wide range of options, including stocks, bonds, money markets, balanced funds, and, in some cases, international equity and fixed income funds.
* A portion of the assets in your variable annuity can also be in-

Exhibit 5-4. How fixed annuities compare to CDs.

A fixed annuity can be thought of a as a tax-deferred CD with an insurance company. To better understand the similarties and differences between CDs and annuities, refer to the following chart.

CD	Fixed Annuity
Lump-sum deposit	Lump sum or multiple deposit
Guaranteed principal	Guaranteed principal
Guaranteed interest rate	Guaranteed interest rate
Simple interest paid by most banks	Compounded interest paid by most insurance carriers
Guaranteed rate period	Guaranteed rate period
Penalty for early withdrawal	Penalty for early withdrawal
Ease of making investment	Ease of making investment
No front-end costs	No front-end costs
Income taxable on Schedule B	Income tax-deferred (until withdrawn)
No annual fees	No annual fees

vested in a fixed account option that functions much like a standard fixed annuity.
* Your original investment is guaranteed to be returned to your heirs in the event of your death.

There are, of course, potential disadvantages of variable annuities:

* Principal in the annuity is subject to market volatility.
* Your income stream may be unstable because the payout depends on the investment performance. If the overall value increases, the monthly check will increase; however, if the account value decreases, so too will the monthly check.

Exhibit 5-5 compares the costs and benefits of mutual funds and variable annuities.

Exhibit 5-5. How mutual funds compare to variable annuities.

Mutual Fund Family	Variable Annuity
Front-end load or no-load	No front-end load
Various funds from which to choose	Various funds from which to choose; Most have a "fixed account" option
Flexibility to switch funds	Flexibility to switch funds without incurring tax liability
Annual management fees	Annual management fees
Distribution expenses	Mortality charges
No annual policy fee	$25–$35 annual policy fee
Mgt. fees = .5–1.0%	Mgt. fees = .5–1.0%
Capital gains/losses-Schedule D	No reporting of capital gains/losses
No mortality (death) benefits	Untimely death "Die in a Down Market" benefit
Must sell shares to make any withdrawal	May annuitize; take payout structure to fit client need

Annuities and Probate

One important characteristic of fixed and variable annuities is that there is no probate upon the death of the contract owner.

This means that the accumulated value of the annuity contract can be passed immediately to the beneficiary without being tied up in probate. What's more, if the beneficiary is the surviving spouse, that person may choose to become the successor owner of the annuity. In this case, the spouse may keep the annuity in force rather than receiving accumulated proceeds.

In the case of variable annuities, a guaranteed death benefit is paid even if the investment account within the annuity has declined in a down market. That's because most variable annuities provide mortality guarantees designed to protect the contract owner in the event of death.

These so-called die-in-a-down-market clauses generally guarantee to return the greater of the following: the market value of the account on the date of death, or the sum of the premium payments. Thus, the original contract owner can be assured of leaving no less than the original premium payments to his or her beneficiaries upon death.

Why Buy an Annuity?

As we have noted, annuities are often ideal for those individuals seeking to save for retirement while reducing their taxable income by deferring taxable gains to a later date. But the appeal of annuities goes beyond the ability to achieve tax-deferred accumulation of assets.

Consider investing in *fixed annuities* if you meet any or all of these tests:

* You want to lock in a set level of interest for an extended period of time.
* You are older than 59½ and seek liquidity in your investments.
* The prospect of having a permanent income stream at retirement greatly appeals to you.
* You would like to avoid probate by passing a large sum of money to an heir by contract.
* You need a conservative component in your investment portfolio.
* You need to supplement your IRA savings. A key advantage of the annuity contract is that it does not limit your annual contributions to $2,000 a year.
* Safety of principal is of paramount importance to you.

Consider investing in *variable annuities* if you meet any or all of these tests:

* Portfolio diversification is important to you.
* You are an investor who seeks to switch your position from one type of investment to another in response to changing market conditions.
* You are determined to keep ahead of the inflationary curve.
* The idea of having a minimum death benefit regardless of market conditions adds to your feelings of financial security.
* You do not need income from your investments prior to age 59½.

Before You Take the Plunge. A fixed annuity should not be purchased on the basis of the interest rate alone. In fact, a number of annuities that appear to offer high interest rates are really less attractive than they appear on the surface.

That's because they are loaded with negative features, including high surrender charges on the withdrawal of cash and the payment of "low-ball" interest rates when contracts are renewed. So when you are presented with a fixed annuity that appears to offer an exceptionally high yield, remember the old adage: "If something looks too good to be true, it probably is."

With this in mind, the best approach is to seek a balance, choosing a contract that offers a competitive interest rate, reasonable withdrawal provisions, favorable surrender charges, and a strong renewal history. The following are key benchmarks in making your selection:

Interest rate:	Strive for 1–1.5% higher than the current CD rate.
Withdrawal provisions:	Look for the right to withdraw 10% of the accumulated value or all of the accumulated interest without penalty from the insurance company. If you are quite certain that you will not need the interest income in the first year of the contract, the interest option is almost always preferable.

For example, assume you have invested $100,000 at 8%:

	End of			
	Year 1	Year 2	Year 3	Year 4
Balance	$108,000	$116,640	$125,971	$136,048
Money Available for Withdrawal:				
At 10%:	$10,800	$11,664	$12,597	$13,604
Interest only:	8,000	16,640	25,971	36,048

Surrender charges:	These should decline over a six-year period from 6% to no charge after the sixth year.
Renewal history:	The insurance company should have a stated policy of crediting the annuity at the new policy rate or a portfolio rate.

One final note: Some annuities allow for subsequent contributions after the initial date of purchase. This may prove beneficial if you have multiple CDs maturing at different times and you want to roll them over into an annuity.

✳ On the Taxpayer Profile, under Lines 8a, 8b, and 9, check Yes if you are invested in CDs and check the appropriate lines that apply to your situation. Also, enter your tax bracket and, if you are in a tax bracket greater than 15%, check the appropriate line to review alternative investments that may provide you with a high after-tax rate of return. If you have no investments, start a monthly savings plan today and review Chapter 1.

Turning an Annuity Into an Income Stream

At some point, you may want to tap into the capital that has accumulated in your annuity to obtain an income stream. With an annuity, this can be done in one of two ways.

The first method is to wait until you reach age 59½, when you may make withdrawals at your discretion. (Withdrawals made before reaching this age may be subject to a 10% penalty tax and will be treated as ordinary income in the year of the withdrawal.)

If you elect to make withdrawals, you retain control over your investment. The downside is that you are not guaranteed a lifetime income stream (one of the key features of an annuity) because your withdrawals may deplete the funds in the annuity contract.

The other way to receive an income stream from your annuity is to annuitize your contract.

When you annuitize, a payment stream based on a systematic liquidation of the investment will be established and guaranteed by the insurance company. When annuitization is elected, you can choose from among these options:

Lifetime income:	Pays monthly installments for as long as you live.
Life income with period certain:	Assures you of monthly income for as long as you live but also goes a step further, assuring a minimum number of payments are made whether you live or die during the guaranteed payment period.
Joint and survivor:	Ensures one monthly check for as long as you (the "annuitant") and a secondary payee are alive. After

one of you dies, the surviving payee continues to receive payments for life (in an equal or adjusted amount, as originally directed).

Income for a specified period: Provides a monthly check for a specified period of time.

Income of a specified amount: Provides a monthly check for a specified sum.

Notes on Annuitization

Caveats Associated With Annuitization

— If the funds in the annuity represent virtually all of your assets, annuitization can deprive you of a liquid fund to cover emergencies. The widely accepted rule of thumb is that you need an emergency cash (or other liquid asset) reserve to cover at least three to five months of living expenses.

— Electing annuitization means you are locked in to an income stream at a set interest rate. Once the payout begins, it cannot be stopped. This can prove disadvantageous in inflationary periods as your income fails to keep pace with rising costs.

— The younger you are, the less monthly income you will receive from annuitization. That's because the payout is based, in part, on life expectancy.

— If you are determined to leave the assets in your annuity to your heirs, then annuitization is not for you. That's because the payouts stop once the annuitant and the second payee die.

Single-premium whole life insurance policies (see Chapter 3) can function much like annuities while allowing you to pass the assets to your heirs income-tax free. As with annuities, single-premium policies offer guaranteed principal and interest rate as well as tax-deferred earnings.

But unlike annuities, the proceeds from a single-premium policy (which include the original premium deposit, the earnings generated in the policy, and a life insurance benefit) pass to a beneficiary on a tax-free basis. Of course, there is no free lunch, and in this case the price to be paid comes in the form of a lower interest rate on the money placed in the life contract. For example, if single-premium annuities are paying 8.75%, a single-premium whole life policy will typically yield 8–8.25%.

Banking on the Insurance Industry

If you are reluctant to invest in annuities because of concern for the financial solvency of the insurance industry, you can limit the risks by investing in only the most stable companies. Consider these steps:

1. *Review the ratings of the various companies.* A. M. Best and Standard & Poor are two of the top independent rating services. Best rates companies on their ability to pay claims, and S&P rates overall financial strength.

2. *Determine how the insurance company invests your money.* Be wary of those carriers heavily invested in high-yield bonds and real estate. Companies maintaining diversified investment philosophies should be in the best position to protect your investment in the event of a severe economic downturn.

3. *Look at the insurers' profitability.* The profitability test measures a company's ability to control its expenses while increasing income.

Review all annuity options and their advantages, disadvantages, and tax implications with your financial advisor.

✽ On the Taxpayer Profile, Line 8b, enter the amount of tax-exempt income from your Form 1040. Check the appropriate boxes to review your after-tax rate of return and your diversification and income requirements.

Chapter 6

From Self-Employment to Social Security—Making Tax-Wise Investments: Lines 12–19, 21, 26, and 27

> The difference between ordinary and extraordinary is that little extra.
>
> Unknown

We now begin discussion of a wide range of tax questions that affect your investment strategy. As you follow along with a copy of your last completed Form 1040 and your Taxpayer Profile, remember: Any poor tax decision or anemic investment has a negative impact on your wealth-building program and, in turn, on your ability to achieve financial independence.

Schedules C, E, and F

The following lines on your 1040, should they apply to you, require the filing of special schedules: Lines 12, 18, and 19 (self-employment income); Line 26 (self-employed health insurance deduction); Line 27 (Keogh retirement plan and self-employed SEP deduction).

The necessary schedules are:

Schedule C: Business income or loss
Schedule E: Partnerships
Schedule F: Farm income or loss

If you have earned income from self-employment or from participating in a partnership, you are required to file one or more of these schedules. This indicates your eligibility to contribute money on a pretax basis to a Simplified Employee Pension plan or to a Keogh plan.

Both of these plans allow for current tax sheltering of income as well as tax-deferred accumulation over the years. If you qualify, this is a great opportunity to reduce current taxes and accelerate your wealth-building program.

Simplified Employee Pensions (SEPs)

A Simplified Employee Pension, as it is formally known, comes in two basic formats: the SEP-IRA and the SAR-SEP.

The SEP-IRA is a simplified employee pension plan through which employer contributions are made to IRA accounts established and maintained by eligible employees. An employer who makes these tax-deductible contributions may not discriminate between high-paid and low-paid workers.

Additional Rules Governing SEP-IRAs

* The maximum contribution is 15% of employee compensation to a maximum of $30,000 per year, or 13.043% of self-employed income less one-half of self-employment tax paid.

* Contributions need not be made every year. They are discretionary and can be based, for example, on the employer's profitability.

* IRS approval is not required to set up a SEP-IRA.

* The plans can be established with an independent trust company, providing for self-directed accounts that give the individual participants the flexibility, through self-directed accounts, to diversify into stocks, bonds, mutual funds, CDs, treasuries, or limited partnerships. Participants can also spread their investments among several different fund families.

* Should the employer make excess contributions to an employee's SEP-IRA in a given year, the employee must withdraw the excess before the tax return due date or be subject to a 6% excise tax. Because the tax obligation falls on the employee, make it the employer's responsibility to confirm that employer contributions do not exceed the maximum sums.

* Once an employer establishes a SEP-IRA, eligible employees must be covered under it. With a few exceptions, eligible employees are those

at least 21 years old and with at least three years of service to the company in the last five years. Employers can opt for less restrictive eligibility.

* You can make withdrawals from an IRA at any time. However, if such withdrawals occur before the employee reaches age 59½, the employee will be subject to a withdrawal penalty of 10% in addition to the ordinary income tax.

With a SAR-SEP (otherwise known as a salary-reduction SEP), employee contributions are made through salary deferral, with the amount deferred put into the SEP. This type of plan is limited to companies with 25 or fewer employees.

As a participant in a SAR-SEP, an employee can set aside up to 15% of his pretax income, to a maximum of $8,994. Wages and other employment earnings invested in an SAR-SEP are shielded from taxation until the funds are withdrawn.

The key difference between SAR-SEPs and SEP-IRAs is this: With an SEP-IRA, only the employer can make contributions to the plan; with the SAR-SEP, both employer and employee can do so. The limitation, however, is that the combined contribution cannot exceed a ceiling of 15% of the employee's compensation to a maximum of $30,000.

Assume, for example, that an employer contributes only 5% of an employee's compensation to a SEP-IRA and the employee would like to set aside more. If the plan is changed to a SAR-SEP, the employee can contribute another 10%, to a maximum of $8,994 in 1993, to the plan on her own behalf. The beauty of the combined contribution is that it increases the employee's wealth-building capability without increasing the cost to her employer.

Money in either type of SEP—which can be invested in a wide range of options, such as stocks, bonds, mutual funds, real estate limited partnerships, and/or precious metals—accumulates on a tax-deferred basis. This makes more dollars available for reinvestment, thus building wealth faster and more substantially than in taxable accounts. Fortunately, the rules governing SEPs are relatively simple (as the name implies), which makes SEPs ideal for the self-employed.

Keoghs

Keogh is the term for qualified plans that are used by unincorporated businesses (i.e., partnerships and sole proprietorships).

Keoghs typically are money-purchase or profit-sharing plans, or both. Under a money-purchase plan, the maximum deductible contribution for the owner is 20% of earned income or $30,000, whichever is less.

If a profit-sharing plan is chosen, a maximum of just over 13% of earned income can be contributed.

Although more complex than SEPs, Keoghs have some important advantages. One benefit of Keoghs to employers is that unlike SEPs, they do not require immediate vesting. This means that employees can be required to work as long as seven years before they have access to their entire contributions. SEP plans generally permit employees to withdraw contributions immediately.

Smaller businesses can enjoy the advantages of a qualified plan through Keoghs. They are well suited to employers who want more than the 15% contribution available from SEPs and do not want immediate vesting.

For a handy guide to Keoghs, SEPs, and other retirement programs, see Appendix B.

✳ Check off answers to the questions on the Taxpayer Profile, Lines 12, 18, 19, and 27, concerning Keoghs and SEPs.

Capital Gains and Losses: Line 13

Line 13 requires the filing of another special form: Schedule D—Capital Gain or Loss.

When it comes to the treatment of capital gains and/or losses, several factors come into play. Although the full amount of a capital gain must be included with your income, it is generally subject to a maximum tax rate of 28%. Moreover, capital gains can be offset by capital losses. If you had $7,000 in capital gains during a given year, for example, and $5,000 in capital losses, you should be able to reduce the gain, for tax purposes, to $2,000.

But what happens if your capital losses exceed your capital gains? Up to $3,000 of the excess loss is deductible in a single year, regardless of the amount of income earned. Additional losses may be nondeductible during that tax year, but they can be carried over to reduce capital gains in subsequent years.

The Tax Swap

Another savvy way to reduce the taxes on capital gains is to engage in so-called tax swaps. The strategy works like this:

Assume you have invested in two bond funds, ABC and XYZ. After being held for more than six months, the ABC investment has produced a paper loss (because you have not sold your shares) of $5,000. At the same time, XYZ has produced a paper gain of $5,000. Because you need the money, or you believe XYZ has gone as high as it will go, you sell the XYZ shares, producing a capital gain of $5,000 subject to current taxation.

In order to shelter that gain from Uncle Sam, you could sell the ABC shares, taking the $5,000 capital loss to offset the XYZ capital gain. Soon after you sell ABC, you buy into another similar bond fund, thus retaining an investment in a like portfolio of fixed-income instruments. In effect, you have "swapped" one bond fund for another in order to create a tax loss sufficient to shelter the XYZ fund capital gain. This strategy can be equally effective for equities.

When tax swapping in individual securities (rather than mutual funds), the trades are simultaneous. The same is true when swapping within a given fund family. But when swapping from one fund to another, there are caveats to consider.

Most important, you must keep in mind that prices can change rapidly and dramatically. For example, during the week following "Black Monday," October 19, 1987, the net asset value (NAV) of quality bond funds rose between 3 and 6%. Hence, an investor liquidating one fund on the prior Friday, with the intention of buying into a similar fund soon after, may have had to pay much more than expected when the purchase was consummated. Remember, the quicker you act, the safer your swap.

Results of Swap

Decrease annual after-tax income by:	$21
Decrease annual par value by:	$5,700
Establish tax loss of:	$23,949
Reduce federal income tax liability by:	$6,706

Make a review of swap opportunities part of your year-end financial planning. Ask your investment advisor to identify swaps that can improve your total return.

✳ On the Taxpayer Profile, Line 13, check off "Consider bond, stock, mutual fund, or UIT tax swaps to create capital losses." If you have assets that should be reviewed for suitability, return, or diversification, check off the appropriate activity.

Rents, Royalties, Partnerships, Estates, and Trusts: Line 18

Line 18 includes various types of earnings. You must complete Schedule E if you have income from any or all of the specified sources. Let's review them briefly, one at a time.

Rental and Royalty Income

This includes all rents from property you own or control as well as royalties from oil, gas or mineral properties, copyrights, and patents.

If you did not play an active role in managing these investments, the so-called **passive** losses generated by these investments generally can now be deducted only to the extent that they offset passive gains. In this context, take a close look at your real return from these assets. Does it make sense to continue to hold them? If the tax benefits that justified the initial purchase are no longer available, a change may be in order.

For example, you may want to invest in **passive income generators**, or PIGs. As the name implies, PIGs produce passive income that can be sheltered with your passive losses. In this way, passive losses (which might otherwise go unused) can be put to work reducing or eliminating the tax bite on other investments.

As you review your Schedule E rental and royalty income, consider selling off the underlying investments or shifting the money to alternative investments to secure higher returns, boost cash flow, gain tax advantages, or simply achieve greater diversification.

Limited Partnerships

Limited partnerships can be excellent vehicles for investing in real estate, equipment leasing, and oil and gas ventures. Successful partnerships offer the opportunity to reap current income and capital gains. What's more, this component of your portfolio can provide a means of effectively outpacing inflation.

Before you select this type of investment, however, a word of caution is in order: Prior to the Tax Reform Act of 1986, limited partnerships were often viewed as potent tax shelters capable of producing tax deductions of several times the actual investment. In that environment, the economic feasibility of many partnerships appeared to be less important than the tax benefits they were touted to deliver.

With the Tax Reform Act, partnership tax benefits were reduced or eliminated (depending on the partnership); now, it is essential that you study an investment's economic viability. Most important, you should make certain that the general partner has a solid track record in delivering solid income and/or strong capital gains.

One more thought on the subject of partnerships: Although investments in partnerships are generally categorized as passive, this need not be the case. For example, you can invest in a *joint venture* or partnership as a general partner that, for tax purposes, is considered a nonpassive working investment. Accordingly, losses generated from this type of investment can be used to offset ordinary income, such as that earned from salary, wages, and tips.

A caution: The general partner in a joint venture or partnership generally does not have the limited liability afforded a limited partner. Accordingly, as a general partner, you could be liable for a pro rata share of the liabilities of the joint venture or partnership.

Estates and Trusts

Estates and trusts generate income which may also be considered passive, thus exposing you to the rules governing passive losses. For this reason, you should explore the use of passive income generators here as well.

In addition, review all of your estate and trust investments with your financial advisor in order to do the following:

* Enhance the potential for current and long-term returns.
* Achieve greater diversification within the estates and trusts and, accordingly, within your overall investment portfolio.
* Reduce the tax burden created by the various investments.

All too often, investments included in estates and trusts are treated as sacrosanct and are thus left as is regardless of their performance. Keep in mind that there is no logical reason for this. The investments should meet the same performance standards as other investments—and should be changed and restructured when they fail to do so.

Remember: Every bad investment, regardless of the form it takes, has a negative impact on your wealth-building program and in turn on your ability to achieve financial independence.

❊ On the Taxpayer Profile, Line 18, answer Yes or No to the questions listed to identify whether you have an asset that needs to be reviewed.

Social Security Benefits: Line 21

It is widely believed that Social Security income is nontaxable. This is true *only* if your income from other sources falls below set levels.

If you are single or married filing separately, and your income from wages, interest income, and other sources plus *one-half* of your Social Security benefits is greater than $25,000, then you must pay taxes on at least some of your benefits. (For those who are married filing joint returns, the income limit before benefits are taxed is $32,000.)

The tax works like this: For every dollar more than $25,000 (or $32,000) earned, 50 cents of your Social Security benefits becomes taxable (Exhibit 6-1). For example, an elderly couple receives $12,000 in Social Security benefits and $20,000 in taxable income. The couple's total income, including benefits, is $32,000, right at the threshold. If the two were to have $12,000 in additional income from savings and investments, then $6,000 of their Social Security benefits, or 50%, would be taxed.

Exhibit 6-1. How to calculate the Social Security benefits tax for an individual.

	Calculating the
	Social Security Benefits Tax
	For an Individual
Combine:	Wages
	+
	Investment Income
	+
	Tax-Exempt Income
	=
	Non-Social Security Income
	+
Add:	1/2 Social Security Benefits
	(including COLA[1] increase)
	−
Substract:[2]	$25,000
	/
Divide:	2
	=
Taxable Benefits:[3]	Total

[1] *Cost of living adjustment.*
[2] *No tax is payable unless the total exceeds $25,000.*
[3] *Treated as taxable income subject to ordinary income tax rate. Maximum taxable benefits are equal to one-half of Social Security benefits.*

In addition to being aware of possible taxation, of course, Social Security recipients under age 70 must be mindful that their earnings could cross certain thresholds that result in the forfeiture of benefits. For single recipients aged 62 to 64 in 1993, every $2 earned over $7,680 results in the loss of $1 in benefits. For those aged 65 to 69, every $3 earned over $10,560 results in the loss of $1.

Regardless of whether or not you will be obligated to pay taxes on your Social Security benefits, your goal in your senior years should be to reduce your overall tax liability. With this in mind, consider the following options:

* *Limited partnerships.* This type of investment can provide a tax-sheltered income stream. The sheltering is achieved when the general partner uses interest expenses and/or depreciation to offset the flow of income produced by the investments. As a senior citizen who has retired or is approaching retirement age, you should limit your investments to partnerships with high safety ratings. This is not the time for speculative filings.

* *Deferred annuities and single-premium whole life insurance policies.* These may be ideal for Social Security recipients whose benefits are taxable and who are in a position to defer all or part of the investment income they are currently receiving. With a single-premium deferred annuity or a single-premium whole life policy, income grows on a tax-deferred basis, returns are guaranteed (except in the case of a variable annuity), and there are no limits on the amounts that can be invested. (See Chapter 5 for additional information on annuities and Chapter 3 for details on whole life policies.)

＊ On the Taxpayer Profile, Line 21, check if you are paying taxes on your Social Security benefits.

Income From Pensions, Annuities, and IRA Distributions: Lines 16a and 17a

Lines 16a and 17a reveal a flow of income from pensions, annuities, profit-sharing plans, employee savings plans, IRA distributions, and IRA rollovers.

The information on these lines plays an important role in creating your wealth-building program. If no income is reported on these lines of your tax return, you should ask yourself, "Why?" Are you eligible for pensions, annuities, IRAs, and the like and simply failing to take advantage of them? If so, you are missing out on an excellent way to build wealth over the years. The fastest and surest route to financial independence is to capitalize on every investment and savings vehicle available to you. (Ask your financial advisor to assess your eligibility.)

If you are reporting income on these lines, meaning you have one or more of the plans in place, analyze your holdings to determine exactly what kinds of assets are held in the plans. Are they suitable for your financial goals? Do they provide an adequate yield or return? Do you have sufficient diversification? Review the assets in your plans in the contexts of risk–reward, diversification, and goal setting.

Determine, too, whether—based on the current distribution rate—there will be adequate funds in the plans to provide a lifetime source of income. If not, you may want to make changes in the assets or the distribution rate.

If you have received distributions this year or in previous years, consider transferring and/or consolidating the assets into a single self-directed plan rather than leaving them scattered in several plans. This can reduce annual maintenance fees and, even more important, can help you to monitor and analyze your investment performance.

Remember, every component of your investment portfolio deserves constant attention and periodic analysis. That's the best way to make certain that your money works as hard as you do.

(IRAs are discussed in further detail in Chapter 7.)

✳ On the Taxpayer Profile, Lines 16a and 17a, check off appropriate activities as they relate to your retirement accounts.

Chapter 7

Using Your Individual Retirement Account to Create Wealth: Line 24

Financial success is never having to balance your checkbook.

Benjamin Graham

Individual Retirement Accounts (IRAs) are an effective vehicle for investing up to $2,000 annually on a tax-advantaged basis. IRA eligibility extends to those earning ordinary employment wages or self-employment income. (It also extends to those receiving alimony payments.)

The extent of the IRA-related tax advantages you can qualify for depends on two key factors: (1) your adjusted gross income and (2) whether you are already covered by a qualified plan offered by an employer. The amount you are able to deduct from your adjusted gross income reduces your taxable income by that amount.

IRA Strategies

If you are not active in a qualified plan, your full IRA contribution (100% of earned income to a maximum of $2,000) can be made on a pretax basis. This means you deduct the amount of the contribution from your adjusted gross income for tax purposes.

For those who are already covered by an employer-sponsored plan, consider the following IRA scenarios (see also Exhibit 7-1):

Exhibit 7-1. How to determine deductibility of an IRA.

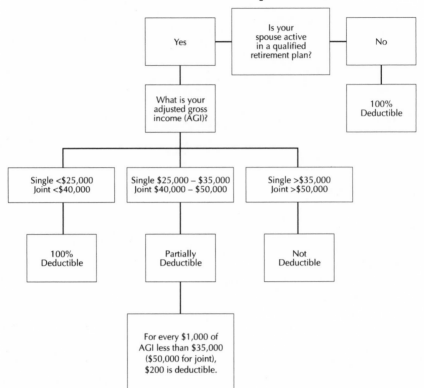

Scenario 1: IRA Contribution Is Totally Deductible

Taxpayer	AGI	IRA Contribution Deductible
Single	Less than $25,000	100%
Joint	Less than $40,000	100%

* *Single taxpayer.* Because you are single and your adjusted gross income (AGI) is under $25,000 a year, you may deduct the total amount of your IRA contribution, up to $2,000, from your AGI, thus reducing your taxable income.

* *Couple filing jointly.* Because you are married and filing jointly and together your combined income is less than $40,000, the IRA contribution is still fully deductible. The maximum contribution of $2,000 each can be used to decrease your taxable income. The limit is $2,250 for a married couple with only one income. This is called a **spousal account**.

Scenario 2: IRA Contribution Is Partially Deductible

Taxpayer	AGI	IRA Contribution Deductible
Single	$25,000–$35,000	$200 for every $1,000 of AGI
Joint	$40,000–$50,000	$200 for every $1,000 of AGI

* *Single taxpayer.* There are several levels of IRA contribution deductibility for single filers with incomes of $25,000 to $35,000. The general rule is that for each $1,000 in AGI under $35,000, you can deduct $200 of your IRA contribution.

* *Couple filing jointly—individual accounts.* There are several levels of IRA contribution deductibility for joint filers with AGIs in the $40,000–$50,000 range. Generally, you can deduct $200 of your IRA contribution for every $1,000 of your AGI under $50,000.

* *Couple filing jointly—spousal account.* For a spousal account, the first 1,000 in AGI under $50,000 (i.e., $49,000) is eligible for a $200 deduction. The next level of income, $48,000, is eligible for a $450 deduction. Thereafter, each $1,000 of income under $48,000 bears a $225 deduction until the maximum deduction of $2,250 is reached at $40,000 AGI.

Scenario 3: IRA Contribution Is Not Deductible

Taxpayer	AGI	IRA Contribution Deductible
Single	Greater than $35,000	No
Joint	Greater than $50,000	No

* *Single taxpayer.* For single filers with income over $35,000, IRA contributions are no longer deductible. You may still make IRA contributions, and although they are not tax deductible, the earnings will still accumulate tax-deferred. In your tax bracket, that can be quite significant.

* *Joint filers.* With a joint AGI of over $50,000, you and your spouse cannot deduct the IRA contribution from your taxes. You may still make IRA contributions, and although they are not tax deductible, the earnings will accumulate tax-deferred, and in your tax bracket that can be quite significant.

As with all long-term investments, even modest increases in annual yields earned on IRA accounts can have a substantial impact on wealth creation (see Exhibit 7-2, which assumes reinvestment of interest and dividends).

Selecting a Trustee

An IRA must be held by a trustee or a custodian, generally a bank, brokerage, or other type of investment firm. Be aware, however, of the critical difference between a trustee acting on behalf of an investment product (including a family of mutual funds) and an independent trustee.

In virtually all cases, the latter is preferable. That's because the independent trustee does not have a self-interest in limiting you to a relatively small group of investments.

An IRA established with an independent trustee is generally a self-directed account that gives you the flexibility to diversify your investment portfolio to include stocks, bonds, mutual funds, certificates of deposit, Treasury bills, limited partnerships, and precious metals—and to select from the universe of available investment products.

IRA Fact Sheet

+ If you qualify to establish an IRA, your nonworking spouse may do the same.

+ Earnings derived from assets—including interest, rents, and dividends—are not considered "compensation" for the purpose of calculating IRA contributions.

+ IRA contributions can be made at any time during the taxable year, up to the federal income tax filing date of April 15 (not including filing extensions).

+ IRA contributions that exceed the maximum annual ceilings are subject to a 6% annual excise tax. However, should the excess contributions (and the earnings generated from them) be withdrawn from the accounts before the federal income tax filing due date, the excise tax will be waived.

+ The costs associated with IRAs are generally modest, including a one-time set-up fee of about $25 or less and annual maintenance fees that typically range from $10 to $50. (Maintenance fees for self-directed accounts can be substantially higher.)

Exhibit 7-2. How yield affects building wealth in IRA accounts.

No. of Years	Cumulative Contribution	Account Value at 8%	Account Value at 10%	Account Value at 12%
5	$ 10,000	$ 12,670	$ 13,430	$ 14,230
10	20,000	31,290	35,062	39,308
15	30,000	58,648	69,898	83,506
20	40,000	98,884	126,004	161,396
25	50,000	157,908	216,362	298,666
30	60,000	244,690	361,886	540,584
35	70,000	372,204	596,252	966,926
40	80,000	559,560	973,702	1,718,284

Built-In Discipline

As we have made clear from the beginning, financial discipline is essential to a successful wealth-building program. If you have trouble mustering the discipline to save, consider using mutual fund check draft privileges to make your IRA contribution in monthly installments. That way, discipline is built-in, since your contribution is automatically withdrawn from your checking account.

Moreover, instead of having to come up with a lump-sum $2,000 payment, you can make your contribution in manageable payments throughout the year. As an additional benefit, making contributions all year rather than waiting until you file your tax return gives you a head start on the compounding phenomenon that works so powerfully over the years.

How powerfully? Investing $2,000 at 12% at the beginning of the year—versus waiting until year's end—brings you an additional $17,000 over a 20-year period. (See Exhibit 7-3 for the value achieved after 25 years at 10% interest in a tax-deferred IRA account, compared to a taxable investment that also earns 10%.)

※ On the Taxpayer Profile, Line 24, check off the question regarding your current year IRA contribution.

Rolling Over Into an IRA

Once an IRA is established, it can be used as a tax shelter of sorts for earnings from lump-sum distributions from employer tax-qualified plans.

Exhibit 7-3. How tax-deferred IRA contributions build over 25 years.

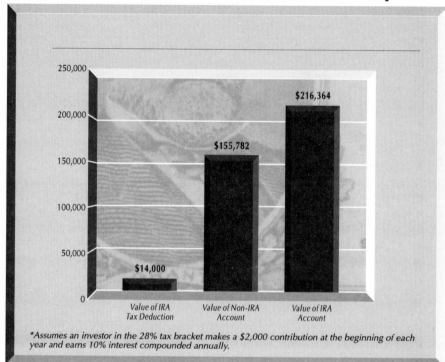

Assumes an investor in the 28% tax bracket makes a $2,000 contribution at the beginning of each year and earns 10% interest compounded annually.

Assume, for example, that you leave your job due to retirement, disability, or cutbacks. If you have funds in the former employer's qualified plan, and these funds are distributed to you, they will be taxed as ordinary income in the year of the distribution. This will create a sudden, and possibly quite large, tax obligation.

To prevent this, you can "roll over" the funds from the employer's qualified plan into an IRA. This prevents the distribution from the employer's plan from triggering a taxable event, and it keeps the funds accumulating in the IRA on a tax-sheltered basis.

Tips on IRA Distributions

You can begin to withdraw money from your IRA at age 59½. Taking money from the fund before then results in a 10% penalty tax over and above the ordinary income tax, unless you are disabled or meet other IRS exceptions.

You *must* withdraw money from your IRA, either as a lump sum or as periodic distributions, beginning at age 70½. When you reach this age, you are no longer eligible to start an IRA.

IRA distributions are generally taxed as ordinary income in the year they are received, although there are exceptions. If you think taxation negates the benefit of the initial deferment, think again: Assuming the funds were contributed on a pretax basis, your tax obligation was reduced and you had more dollars available to invest.

Also, whether the contributions are deductible or nondeductible, funds in the IRA account accumulate on a tax-deferred basis, meaning more money is available for reinvestment. Additionally, by the time you must take IRA withdrawals, chances are good that you will be in a lower tax bracket than when the contributions were made—resulting in a smaller take for Uncle Sam.

IRA withdrawals may be taken in a number of formats:

* As a lump sum distribution
* As regular payments over the joint lives or life expectancies of you and your designated beneficiary
* As an annuity purchased with the money in the IRA, payable over the joint lives or life expectancy of you or your beneficiary
* As annuity or regular payments taken over any length of time less than the life expectancy of yourself or your beneficiary

Regardless of which payout option you choose, the minimum annual withdrawal after age 70½ cannot be less than the amount obtained by dividing the value of the IRA by your life expectancy or by the joint life expectancies of yourself and your designated beneficiary.

The valuation of the IRA is its market value on December 31 of the year you reach age 70½. Take care to structure the withdrawal amounts so that you do not fall below the minimum sums required by law. Should you do so, the government will impose a 50% excise tax on the shortfall.

※ On the Taxpayer Profile, lines 16a, 17a, and 24, check off questions regarding rollovers, IRA consolidation, and early funding in monthly installments.

Chapter 8

Itemized Deductions and What They Reveal About You: Line 34

Money is just something to make bookkeeping convenient.

H. L. Hunt

The deductions you claim on your Schedule A, which you must fill out in addition to Line 34 when you choose to itemize, can reveal a great deal about the way you manage—or, in many cases, *mis*manage—your finances.

Are You Paying Too Much Interest?

Although no longer deductible, the amount of interest you pay could indicate that you have overextended yourself with bank loans or credit card borrowing and, hence, are overburdened with interest charges. This is more than a painful obligation: It is a detour on the road to financial independence. The more you are borrowing, and are thus required to repay, the less you have to invest in your wealth-building program.

"Well, then," you may now be asking, "how do I know if I'm in over my head?"

Computing Your Debt-to-Income Ratio

The first step toward eliminating debt is to find out exactly how much debt you have in relation to your income. As a general rule, if your debt is 15% of your income or less, you are in relatively good shape. Should your obligations fall between 15 and 20% of your income, be careful; you could be getting in over your head. If your debt is greater than 20% of your income, you have lost control and should take action immediately to reduce what you owe.

To compute your debt-to-income ratio, complete the following worksheets.

Add Up Your Debt

Creditor*	Monthly Payment	Last Month's Interest Charge
1. _____	$_____	$_____
2. _____	$_____	$_____
3. _____	$_____	$_____
4. _____	$_____	$_____
5. _____	$_____	$_____
6. _____	$_____	$_____
7. _____	$_____	$_____
8. _____	$_____	$_____
9. _____	$_____	$_____
10. _____	$_____	$_____
11. _____	$_____	$_____
Total:	$_____	$_____

*Do not include mortgage or rent.

Add the two totals together and use this figure as the total monthly debt payment in the following formula; then compute your debt-to-income ratio.

Total monthly debt payment
except mortgage
÷Monthly after-tax income = debt-to-income ratio

The Debt Check

If your debt-to-income ratio is greater than 15%, it's time to rethink your approach to credit. To assess the seriousness of your debt problem, take the following quiz:

	Yes	No
1. Are you using money from your savings to pay your bills?	___	___
2. Are you borrowing to pay for things you used to buy with cash?	___	___
3. Are you able to maintain an adequate emergency fund of at least three months' take-home pay?	___	___
4. Can you make only the minimum payments on your revolving charge accounts?	___	___
5. Are you uncertain how much you owe?	___	___
6. Are you waiting 60 or 90 days to pay bills you used to pay within 30 days?	___	___
7. Are you generally late paying your bills?	___	___
8. Are you nearing the limit on your lines of credit, with no realistic game plan for reducing your debt?	___	___
9. Do you face harassment by creditors, repossession of your car, or other legal action?	___	___

An affirmative response to any of questions 1 through 3 may be an initial warning sign that your financial house is not in order. If you answered yes to question 4, 5, or 6, you should put a temporary halt to credit use and develop a realistic household budget. A yes to any of the last three questions is bad news; you are in trouble and should seek credit counseling immediately.

Managing Your Debt

To control your debt and get back on the path to financial freedom, consider the following suggestions:

* *Be wary of credit cards.* Overuse of credit cards is a costly habit. What may appear at the time of purchase to be "plastic power" turns out later to be "plastic poison" that, if relied on to excess, overwhelms your finances and impedes wealth building.

With this in mind, try to limit credit card purchases to those emergencies when you find yourself with no cash and no alternative method of payment.

Using cash instead of credit cards helps you to manage your debt load in two ways:

1. You may think twice about shelling out $50 for dinner when you have to pay in cash rather than by credit card. This may give you the discipline to curb unnecessary nights on the town and other discretionary spending (ties, perfume, clothing).
2. By limiting your credit card charges, you will be limiting your interest expenses. To get the most out of this, create a "slush fund" of, say, 20% of your monthly living expenses. When you need a new refrigerator or a battery for your car, dip into the cash fund rather than using your credit card.

Think of the benefits you will gain: You will collect interest from the slush fund rather than paying it to the credit card companies.

* *Avoid long-term car payments.* When financing an automobile purchase, resist the temptation to reduce monthly payments by stretching out the term of the loan or the lease. The longer you pay for the car, the more you will be paying in financing costs. A good rule of thumb is to avoid financing terms that are longer than the length of time you plan to keep the car (or other financed asset).

* *Consider debt consolidation.* Should you find yourself in over your head, explore the advantages of a debt consolidation loan. This will not reduce your outstanding payments, but it may enable you to convert your debt to a lower interest rate, thus reducing the overall cost of the credit card charges and other borrowings.

For assistance, ask your tax accountant for the name of a reputable debt counselor or find out if this service is available from your employer.

Tax Breaks for Borrowers

If you have debt, manageable or otherwise, be sure to take advantage of the tax breaks that allow borrowers to deduct their interest payments. These write-offs can help to subsidize some of your debt, reducing your taxes and freeing up more money for investment.

Interest may be fully deductible, totally nondeductible, or deductible subject to restrictions:

Fully Deductible (Generally)

+ Home mortgage on first and second homes
+ Trade or business

Nondeductible

− Personal
− Related to tax-exempt activities

Deductible Subject to Restrictions

* Passive activity (limited by the passive activity rules)
* Investment (limited to the amount of investment income)
* Retirement plan loans (may be limited depending on type of retirement plan)

Fully Deductible Interest

* *Business or trade debt.* The interest in borrowing for business activities, including loans to buy plant and equipment, is generally deductible.

* *Qualified housing debt.* Interest on the mortgage debt incurred in acquiring a primary or a secondary residence is fully deductible (up to $1 million of debt). Important: Primary or secondary mortgages acquired prior to October 13, 1987, are still considered acquisition debt; therefore, the interest related to these mortgages is fully deductible, *regardless of the amount.*

Interest on up to $100,000 of home equity debt in excess of the acquisition debt is also fully deductible, regardless of how the proceeds are used. Although the deductibility of home equity loans makes this type of borrowing highly attractive, there is a major risk involved. If the debt proves unmanageable, you stand the chance of losing what is likely your most precious asset: your house.

This risk increases when the home equity financing is tied to an adjustable rate. An interest cost that seems manageable at 10% may, if rates rise dramatically over the term of the financing, prove to be a terrible burden at 15%. To safeguard yourself from getting into a situation where your house is at risk, project the highest level to which interest rate charges could reasonably climb and see how this figures into your budget. If a serious problem could lie ahead, forget the home equity loan—tax advantages or not.

Interest Deductible With Restrictions

* *Investment debt.* This is money borrowed for use in a nonbusiness venture that is designed, nevertheless, to generate profit. For the most part, this means debt incurred for investment purposes, such as the purchase of stock. Interest expenses resulting from this borrowing are deductible *only* to the extent that they offset investment income.

Nondeductible Interest

* *Consumer debt.* Money borrowed for assets or activities unrelated to a trade or business is consumer debt. This includes loans for the purchase of personal automobiles, home improvement loans, and credit card purchases for clothing, vacations, housewares, and the like. The interest paid on this type of debt ceased to be deductible as of January 1, 1991.

Tips on Consumer Debt

Because the tax rules governing consumer debt were tightened to virtually eliminate deductions, we recommend that you begin a systematic process of paying off consumer debts, beginning with those loans carrying the highest interest rates (most likely your credit card balances).

As a related strategy, limit your use of credit cards so that you are able to pay the balance in full within the billing period. This gives you the convenience of making credit purchases without paying the high interest rates generally associated with them.

When the interest on your debt is significant, but your investment income is not, you might consider restructuring part of your portfolio to generate more current income, as opposed to long-term capital gains. This will make otherwise taxable income nontaxable.

If you are a business owner and have the option to finance a legitimately business-related asset personally or through the business, you should conduct the transaction through the business. This will permit you to take advantage of the deductibility of business interest.

One last tip: Consider refinancing your home mortgage if prevailing interest rates are at least two points below your current mortgage rate. Even though you will have to pay closing costs—which may offset the lower interest costs in the first year or two—over the longer term the savings may be significant. Simply reducing your mortgage payment by $100 a month provides you with another $1,200 a year to invest in your wealth-building program.

To make certain the funds are used in this manner, consider having a mutual fund withdraw the money automatically from your checking account. This way, your monthly budget will remain the same, but you will be accomplishing dual goals: paying off your mortgage and adding to your investment portfolio—clearly a win/win situation.

Wait, There's More

Line 34 is discussed further in Chapter 9, where you will learn how to maximize your itemized deductions to reduce your overall tax burden.

❋ On the Taxpayer Profile, Line 34, check the boxes as they apply to your particular financial situation.

Chapter 9

Tax Refunds and Tax Reduction: Lines 10, 34, and 62

> The income tax has made more liars out of the American people than golf has.
>
> Will Rogers

Typically, a tax refund ignites a celebration. You rush out to spend the refund on a discretionary purchase or a series of purchases—new clothing, a night on the town, maybe even a European vacation. The feeling that this is "found money" prompts you to indulge.

But, wait a minute. This isn't really "found money." It is a refund of excess taxes you have paid.

Rather than engage in self-indulgence, you'd be wiser to use the proceeds to do any of the following:

1. *Add the money to an existing mutual fund account or other personal investment.* Salting away an extra $1,000 a year in tax refunds can produce $98,347 over a 25-year period (figuring a 10% annual return).

2. *Start an investment portfolio or savings account.*

3. *Pay off existing debts.* The more you clear away costly debt—such as credit card balances—from your personal balance sheet, the more of your income you can direct toward wealth-building investments.

4. *Contribute to your individual retirement account.* Even if the contribution must be made with after-tax dollars, the invested tax return will com-

Many of the strategies outlined in this chapter were excerpted from *Year-End Tax Guides,* produced by Practice Development Institute, 401 N. Michigan Avenue, Suite 2600, Chicago, Illinois, 60030; (800) 227-0498.

pound on a tax-deferred basis. This puts your refund to effective use, accelerating your drive toward financial independence.

An Interest-Free Loan for Uncle Sam

A better long-term strategy is to reduce your tax withholding. The reason: A tax refund really amounts to a thank-you from Uncle Sam for overpaying your taxes and providing the government with an interest-free loan.

If you received a refund on your last return, reassess your withholding for the current year. An adjustment can increase your paycheck—giving you your "found money" earlier so that you can invest it over the course of the year.

Adjusting your withholding is easy and can be done at any time. Simply check one of your pay stubs to determine the amount of taxes being withheld for federal income tax purposes each week; then, multiply this figure by the number of times you are paid annually to estimate the total amount that will be withheld during the tax year.

Compare this figure with your tax liability last year. If your current-year's withholding covers last year's liability (or at least 90% of your estimated tax liability for the current year), the IRS cannot generally penalize you for underwithholding.

If much more than this amount is being withheld, it might be wise for you to complete a new Form W-4. You may be entitled to additional allowances, such as those for itemized deductions, that can increase your take-home pay, giving your investments more time to work for you.

✳ On the Taxpayer Profile, Lines 10 and 62, check off whether you expect to receive a tax refund. Indicate which activity would be appropriate in your particular situation.

Of course, while it is usually a good strategy to maximize your take-home pay, increasing what you take home is only half the battle: you also want to *keep* as much of your money at home as possible.

The following sections discuss specific strategies for deferring income and maximizing itemized deductions. There is also an overview of the **alternative minimum tax.**

Strategies for Maximizing Deductions

In Chapter 8, we discussed how itemized deductions showcase your level of debt. Of course, Line 34 of Form 1040 also provides you with myriad possibilities for reducing taxes. In Chapter 8, we showed you how to deduct interest on your debts. Now you will learn the rules governing medical, state income tax, charitable, and miscellaneous deductions.

Various itemized deductions have been limited for the past several years, and those limitations are still applicable. Starting in 1991, deductions (other than medical, casualty and theft losses, and investment interest) were further reduced by 3% of the amount of adjusted gross income in excess of $100,000. Taxpayers cannot lose more than 80% of these itemized deductions. Exhibit 9-1 reveals the average itemized deductions across several income levels and categories of deductions.

Medical Deductions

To maximize your medical deductions, we suggest you:

1. *Bunch expenses.* Deductions are limited to the amount exceeding 7.5% of adjusted gross income. To exceed the floor, you might have to bunch expenses in one year. For example, if you have flexibility as to when you pay your bills or schedule elective surgery or medical appointments, you may be able to use this strategy.

Exhibit 9-1. Average itemized deductions.
Source: Research Institute of America

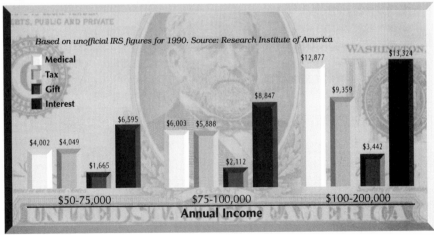

Based on unofficial IRS figures for 1990. Source: Research Institute of America

Medical
Tax
Gift
Interest

$4,002 $4,049 $1,665 $6,595 — $50-75,000
$6,003 $5,888 $2,112 $8,847 — $75-100,000
$12,877 $9,359 $3,442 $13,324 — $100-200,000

Annual Income

2. *Claim medical expenses for nondependents.* Even if you cannot claim a child or parent as an exemption, you can still deduct medical expenses paid for them if you provide more than half their support.

3. *Deduct insurance premiums.* Health and dental insurance premiums as well as Medicare premiums are all deductible. Life and replacement-of-lost-earnings insurance premiums are not deductible.

4. *Deduct health insurance if self-employed.* You may be able to deduct up to 25% of the amount paid for yourself, your spouse, and your dependents. This deduction is available to the self-employed even if total medical expenses do not exceed 7.5% of adjusted gross income. No deduction is allowed if the taxpayer is eligible to participate in any subsidized health plan of an employer or of a spouse's employer. Partners and salaried shareholders of S corporations also can qualify for this deduction.

5. *Claim qualifying nursing home expenses.* The cost of medical care in a long-term care facility, including meals and lodging, is deductible if the main reason for being in the facility is to get medical care. Meals and lodging are not deductible if the main reason for being there is for "retirement" purposes.

One medical note: Cosmetic surgery is no longer deductible.

State Income Taxes

State income taxes are deductible. You should usually make your fourth quarter state estimated tax payment in December rather than January to make it deductible in the current year. (Do not use this strategy if you are subject to the alternative minimum tax.)

Charitable Deductions

It is better to give than to receive, of course. But it doesn't hurt to receive a tax break when you give, either. Our recommendations:

1. *Accelerate contributions.* Consider accelerating your 1994 contributions into 1993 to receive a deduction this year instead of next.

2. *Establish a charitable trust.* A **charitable remainder trust** provides income to individual beneficiaries. At the end of the term of the trust, the remaining principal goes to charity. A **charitable lead trust** distributes income to charity. At the end of the term of the trust, the remaining principal is distributed to individual beneficiaries. Both types of trusts provide

a partial benefit to charity. Government tables determine the size of the current charitable deduction for the "partial" gift.

3. *Donate appreciated property.* If you donate appreciated property, you receive a deduction equal to the fair market value of the gift, and you avoid paying capital gains tax on the appreciation. You must have held the asset for more than one year, and, in most cases, you must not be subject to the AMT.

Miscellaneous Deductions

"Miscellaneous" expenses are deductible only to the extent that they exceed 2% of adjusted gross income. Consider bunching these expenses in one year, if possible, to exceed the floor.

Partial List of Miscellaneous Expenses

* Employment-related education
* Investment expenses
* Professional dues
* Unreimbursed employee business expenses
* Tax return preparation
* Business periodicals
* IRA fees (if separately billed)
* Safe deposit box
* Tax planning fees
* Union dues
* Tools and supplies
* Job search costs

Strategies for Deferring Income

You can also reduce your taxes by adopting strategies before year-end that defer income. Here are some options:

1. *Maximize retirement plan deposits.* Subject to limitations, the maximum deductible contributions to various retirement plans are:

IRA:	$ 2,000
Spousal IRA:	2,250
401(k):	8,994
Defined contribution plan:	30,000

2. *Defer bonuses and compensation.* If you can, have your year-end bonus delayed until January. Regular compensation can be deferred with a written agreement, entered into *prior* to the time that compensation is

earned. You cannot have any access to or control over the deferred pay until you receive it.

3. *Delay billing.* If you are a self-employed taxpayer on the cash method of accounting, consider delaying your billing as year-end approaches.

4. *Delay collecting rents.* If you are a landlord on the cash method of accounting, consider delaying your billing as year-end approaches.

5. *Consider tax shelters.* If you will have net passive activity income for the year, you can invest in a passive activity that will generate passive losses before year-end. (See Chapter 6 for a discussion.)

6. *Shift income to children.* Gifts of property will shift the tax burden. You can give as much as $10,000 annually to any number of individuals without owing any gift tax. If your spouse joins in the gift, you can transfer $20,000 annually. Any income earned on the property after the transfer is taxable to the recipient. This strategy could also reduce your future estate tax.

The kiddy tax requires children under age 14 with unearned income (e.g., interest and dividends) to pay tax at their parents' highest bracket on any unearned income over $1,100. For this reason, saving taxes by shifting income to young children is difficult. However, the following strategies may still work:

* Because earned income, such as a salary, is not subject to the kiddy tax, consider hiring your child in your business.
* Invest in low-dividend growth stocks that your child would hold at least until age 14.
* Invest in municipal bonds, which are exempt from federal tax to owners of any age.
* Invest in U.S. savings bonds that mature after the child reaches age 14.
* Take advantage of the fact that children over age 14 can have as much as $20,350 taxable income and be in only the 15% tax bracket.

The Alternative Minimum Tax

The alternative minimum tax (AMT) exists to prevent taxpayers from using deductions, exclusions, and credits to avoid paying tax. Taxpayers are required to compute their tax liability using both the regular approach and the AMT method and pay the higher tax.

Why do you need to understand the AMT? Here are two reasons:

1. Certain deductions are not used in determining the AMT, so your taxable income for AMT purposes may be higher.
2. The AMT rate, a flat 24%, is lower than many taxpayer's regular marginal rates.

Computing the AMT

The AMT calculation is a complicated one, but you can get a reasonable estimate of it by starting with your regular taxable income and adding back amounts for certain items that are deductible for regular tax purposes. These items include personal exemptions, state and local taxes, miscellaneous itemized deductions, and a portion of medical expenses (only expenses exceeding 10% of AGI are allowed).

The AMT rate is a flat 24% of AMT income exceeding a $30,000 exemption for single taxpayers and $40,000 exemption for taxpayers filing jointly. The exemption is phased out at specific levels of income (see Exhibit 9-2).

The AMT Credit

The AMT is not always as bad as it may seem. A credit is available when the AMT is caused by modifications that merely defer the regular tax (e.g., accelerated depreciation) as opposed to items that permanently avoid the regular tax (such as taxes and miscellaneous itemized deductions). The credit can be used in future years to the extent the regular tax exceeds the AMT.

Exhibit 9-2. How the AMT works.

	Regular Tax	AMT
Regular taxable income	$ 100,000	$ 100,000
Add-back for AMT:		
Personal exemptions		8,600
Taxes		22,000
Misc. itemized deductions		15,000
Less AMT exemption		< 40,000>
Taxable income		
(regular or AMT)	$ 100,000	$ 105,600
TAX	$ 24,116	$ 25,344

These married taxpayers filing jointly with two additional dependents pay $1,228 more due to the AMT.

Chapter 10

Protecting Your Wealth— Estate Planning

> I've got all the money I'll ever need—if I die by four o'clock.
>
> Henny Youngman

Many Americans spend most of their working lives trying to figure out ways to pay less in income tax. They go to great lengths to shelter money with houses, annuities, and tax-free bonds so that their assets will not be raided by the tax collector.

It is ironic that with all the effort exhausted on trying to save taxes while living, most individuals completely ignore the largest tax liability they will ever have to pay—the federal estate tax.

The critical goal of our wealth-building program is to help you achieve financial independence. Our objective is to build a portfolio of assets that can assure you the better things in life: a fine home, quality education for your children, the vacations of your dreams, comfortable retirement—all built on a bedrock of financial security.

In pursuit of these goals, you will try to accumulate a pool of assets—homes, jewelry, cash, investments—that can be passed on to your heirs to help assure your spouse, and ultimately your children, of the continued benefits of your wealth. But to achieve this long-term goal, you must not only save and invest wisely on an ongoing basis but gain an understanding of shrewd and effective estate planning.

You may be shocked to learn that for all your efforts to save and invest wisely during your life, poor estate planning could mean an immediate loss of 37–55% of your total wealth to taxation when you die.

Essentially, estate planning is tax planning. Through proper estate planning, you can reduce estate taxes and provide funds so that estate taxes can be paid without the liquidation of assets.

The Federal Estate Tax

Whereas the income tax affects only the income earned in a particular year, the estate tax applies to the market value of all assets on either the date of death or six months from death, assuming a special alternative valuation date is elected. Thus, the estate tax is generally the largest tax bill an individual will ever receive.

Not everyone will owe federal estate taxes. The government allows each person sufficient credit under the unified estate and gift tax to avoid tax on up to $600,000 of assets upon death. The tax on assets in excess of $600,000 starts at 37% and gets as large as 55% on estates valued at over $3 million. *Thus a large estate could realize a 55% shrinkage if proper planning is not implemented prior to death.*

The effect of the federal estate tax cannot be overestimated. The tax is due nine months from the date of death, which can create significant problems for the survivors of the deceased. For example, if the estate is illiquid (substantially comprised of such holdings as real estate, antiques, or art collections), assets must be sold in order to raise the necessary cash to pay the tax. In these "fire sale" situations, buyers are generally not willing to pay market value. Thus, additional estate shrinkage may take place simply as a result of a forced sale of assets.

In addition to the federal estate tax that may be due upon death, administrative and probate costs may cause further shrinkage.

An individual need not concede to the payment of excessive federal estate taxes. In fact, there are several techniques that can be used to reduce or eliminate entirely the impact of these taxes. It should be noted that all of these strategies involve proper coordination of the services of your tax and financial professionals as well as of your legal counsel.

The Will

The basis of a good estate plan is generally a properly executed will. A will is used to distribute an estate according to the desire of the deceased. A will is also used to name guardians for minor children and to appoint persons to take care of various estate matters. For estates valued at less than $600,000, a will may be the only estate plan necessary. Remember, assets left to heirs by will are subject to probate. This could lead to estate settlement costs beyond the federal estate tax.

The following are the key provisions of a properly structured will:

I. Introduction. *Identifies the testator of the will, establishes residence at the time of execution, and revokes all prior wills.*

II. Family and Property Identification. *Identifies the testator's family and the property passing under the will.*

III. Appointment of Executors. *Appoints an executor and successor executors.* It should be clear that the executor serves independently of court control under the simplified probate administration procedure provided by the laws of certain states. Further, the will should say that the executor serves without fiduciary bond if that is desired. An executor may be appointed to serve alone or in conjunction with some other person or entity. A decision whether an executor receives compensation should be stated.

IV. Appointment of Trustees. *Necessary if a trust is created under the will.* The trustee and successor trustees should be selected and the trustee powers described. Simply referencing the powers provided in the applicable state trust law will provide extensive powers to the trustees. The will should state whether the trustee serves alone or in conjunction with a co-trustee, whether the trustee receives compensation, and whether the trustee will serve without fiduciary bond. A procedure for removal of a trustee should also be set forth, as well as a procedure for the nonjudicial appointment of future trustees.

V. Appointment of Guardians. *Appoints a legal representation for minor children.* A provision for successor guardians should be included, as should a determination about whether the guardian will be compensated or reimbursed for expenses.

VI. Dispositive Provisions. *Describes the disposition of the testator's property.* The property can be disposed of in specific or in general terms, outright, through life estate and remainder interests, and through trusts, whether contained in the will or in a separate document. Powers granted to the testator to appoint property can be exercised under the dispositive provisions of the will. A sweeping residue provision, to encompass all unnamed property, should be placed in this part.

VII. Debts and Administrative Expenses. *Sets forth instructions concerning payment of debts and administration expenses, including the beneficiaries to which the expenses will be charged.*

VIII. Death Taxes. *Provides for the payment of death taxes, including the beneficiary to whom the taxes will be charged.*

IX. Miscellaneous. *Addresses miscellaneous matters that should be covered in a will.* This part should include a statement that the will is not contractual with another will. A clear definition of children and descendants should be set forth, including whether adoptive children and stepchildren will be included. A survivorship requirement also should be set forth. Some wills include a clause that states that a beneficiary who contests the will shall receive no benefits under the will.

X. Testator's Execution. *Deals with testator's statements affirming the will and containing a place for testator's signature to the will.*

XI. Witnesses' Execution. *Deals with statements of witnesses to the will and contains a place for the witnesses to sign the will.*

Probate

Probate is the process that establishes the authenticity or validity of a will. This process is administered through a probate court. Individuals can generally handle the probate of small or simple estates without the assistance of an attorney. Larger, more complicated estates would benefit from the help of an attorney. Probate costs vary from state to state and are affected by the size of the estate and the amount of legal assistance.

For example, a small estate that does not require any legal assistance may cost no more than $500 to probate. On the other hand, probating a large estate with the help of an attorney can cost thousands of dollars.

When probate begins, a number of housekeeping functions are set in motion. A court determines the legitimacy of your will; an executor (designated in your will) is appointed; assets are collected; death taxes, debts, and expenses are paid. Ultimately, the executor distributes assets according to your will with the court supervising the process.

As part of this process, the court issues **letters of administration** or **letters of testamentary** that allow the executor or the administrator (the latter being designated if there is no will or the will is deemed to be invalid) to collect and properly deal with the assets in the estate.

To accomplish this, the executor or administrator takes a complete inventory of the assets and advertises that the estate is being settled. This is done to publicly identify the executor or administrator, to alert creditors and other claimants that the estate is being settled, and to provide a due date for filing claims. The administrator or executor also files claim forms for life insurance, employee benefits, Social Security, veteran's benefits, and other similar benefits to which the estate is entitled.

The executor or administrator is also responsible for the ongoing maintenance of the real property and business interests in the estate. These duties include maintaining insurance contracts, collecting receipts and paying the bills of the business, and honoring buy-sell agreements.

Avoiding Probate

The probating of a will permits a court of law to supervise the transfer of assets from the decedent to his heirs. A typical probate lasts about one year, with six months being a minimum time if everything proceeds smoothly.

Because of the attorney fees, executor's commissions, court costs, and time delay, many people attempt to avoid probate administration.

Methods of Avoiding Probate

* *Joint tenancy.* A form of title arrangement, usually between spouses, where title passes automatically to the surviving joint tenant. There may be income tax disadvantages, and the joint tenancy must be dissolved after one tenant dies.

Another drawback to this arrangement is that creditors of either joint tenant can attach the assets. It may also frustrate estate tax savings, which are anticipated from carefully drafted wills and trusts.

* *Totten Trust.* A method of passing savings accounts to heirs. Passbook accounts are held in trust for another. Typical wording would be: "John Brown, in Trust for John Brown, Jr."

* *Life insurance.* The proceeds of life insurance are rarely subject to probate administration unless the insured's estate is the beneficiary of the policy.

* *Lifetime gifts.* All gifts, even gifts made shortly prior to death, will avoid probate. However, they may be brought back into the estate for death tax purposes.

Also, lifetime gifts carry the donor's basis to the donee, whereas appreciated assets that remain in the decedent's estate will generally get a new or stepped-up basis.

* *Revocable living trusts.* In most situations, the revocable living trust is the best method of avoiding probate. It has the additional advantage of providing management of the funds for the heirs for some time after the decedent's demise. Also, in the event the person setting up the living trust (also called an inter vivos trust) becomes mentally incompetent or otherwise incapacitated, the successor trustee can take over management of the estate.

A living trust is sometimes described as a "will substitute." Like a will, a living trust allows an individual to transfer property to beneficiaries at death. Living trusts have several advantages over wills. First, they allow for the maintenance of the estate in the event of mental incapacitation. Second, a living trust allows assets to pass directly to beneficiaries outside of probate, thereby avoiding probate cost and delays. Third, the provisions of a trust are kept confidential, unlike a will, which is a matter of public record.

Although wills and living trusts serve as the basis of a good estate plan, they do not reduce the size of the estate and, therefore, do not serve to reduce estate taxes.

Reducing Your Estate Tax

Just how the federal tax is applied is illustrated by the case of Cindy Hooper, a single female with a gross estate of approximately $2 million at the time of her death. Funeral and administrative expenses total approximately $74,000, and debts and taxes total about $80,000. See Exhibit 10-1 for how her estate tax liability is figured. Exhibit 10-2 reveals the federal estate and gift tax rates.

A nearly universal goal of estate planning is to limit the estate's tax liability, thus allowing more of the assets to pass to your heirs. Here are some strategies for reducing your estate tax.

Gifting

Current law allows each person to give up to $10,000 per year to any other person without incurring a gift tax. Any gifts in excess of $10,000 are used to reduce the $600,000 estate exclusion discussed above. Although gifts can be used to reduce the size of an estate prior to death, they may not be very effective in the reduction of a very large estate.

Testamentary Trusts

Many estate planning strategies involve the use of trusts. Put simply, a trust is a contract between one party (the grantor) and a second party (the trustee) whereby the trustee agrees to manage the grantor's property for the benefit of a third party (the beneficiary). Trusts may be created during your lifetime (a living trust) or in your will (a testamentary trust).

A testamentary trust is created upon death and can be used effectively to accept the $600,000 estate exclusion and to distribute these assets directly to heirs. In addition, a testamentary trust can be used to pass assets to a surviving spouse without current estate taxation. Any assets passed to a surviving spouse will be taxed upon the death of that spouse.

Exhibit 10-1. How to compute the federal estate tax: example of Cindy Hooper.

	STAGE 1	(1) Gross Estate		$ 2,000,000
minus				
		(2) Funeral and administration expenses	$ 74,000	
		(3) Debt and Taxes	$ 80,000	
		(4) Losses	$	
		Total deductions	$ 154,000	
minus		(5) Adjusted gross income		$ 1,846,000
	STATE 2			
minus		(6) Marital deduction	$ 0	
		(7) Charitable deductions	$ 0	
		Total deductions	$ 0	
equals		(8) Taxable estate		$ 1,846,000
	STAGE 3			
plus		(9) Adjusted taxable gifts (post-1976 lifetime taxable transfers not included in gross estate)	$ 100,000	
equals		(10) Tentative tax base (total of taxable estate and adjusted taxable gift)		$ 1,946,000
com-pute		(11) Tentative tax	$ 756,500	
minus		(12) Gift taxes which would have been payable on post 1976 gifts	$	
equals		(13) Estate tax payable before credit		$ 756,500
	STAGE 4			
minus		(14) Tax credits (a) Unified credit $ 192,800 (b) State death tax credit $ (c) Credit for foreign death taxes $ (d) Credit for tax on prior transfers $ Total reduction $ 192,800		
equals		(15) Net federal estate tax payable		$ 563,700
	STAGE 5			
plus		15% tax on excess accumulations from qualified plans and IRAs		$ 0
	STAGE 6			
equals		(17) TOTAL FEDERAL ESTATE TAX		$ 563,700

Exhibit 10-2. Unified tax schedule for 1989 and after: federal estate and gift tax.

Amount of Adjusted Taxable Estate* or Taxable Gift		Tax Before Deducting Credits	
More Than (1)	Less Than or Equal to (2)	Tax on Amount in Column (1) (3)	Rate of Tax on Excess in Column (1) (4)
$ 0	$ 10,000	0	18%
10,000	20,000	1,800	20
20,000	40,000	3,800	22
40,000	60,000	8,200	24
60,000	80,000	13,000	26
80,000	100,000	18,200	28
100,000	150,000	23,800	30
150,000	250,000	38,800	32
250,000	500,000	70,800	34
500,000	750,000	155,800	37
750,000	1,000,000	248,300	39
1,000,000	1,250,000	345,800	41
1,250,000	1,500,000	448,300	43
1,500,000	2,000,000	555,800	45
2,000,000	2,500,000	780,800	49
2,500,000+		1,025,800	50
For years before 1993			
2,500,000	3,000,000	1,025,800	53
3,000,000+		1,290,800	55

*Adjusted Taxable Estate=Taxable Estate plus post-1976 taxable gifts.
The Tax Reform Act of 1986 has frozen the maximum estate and gift tax rate to 55 for years through 1992.

Note: Beginning with gifts made and estates of persons dying after December 31, 1988, a 5% additional tax is imposed on taxable gifts and taxable estates over $10 million, until the benefit of the unified credit and the graduated rates is completely eliminated. This occurs at $21,040,000 for transfers through the end of 1992. Once the taxable gift or taxable estate reaches $21,040,000, the tax rate is effectively a flat 55%.

Charitable Giving

Current law allows an individual to make unlimited gifts to charity. These gifts provide a direct offset to the size of the estate and thus can be used effectively to reduce estate taxes. The charitable gift is irrevocable: Once made, it can never revert back to the giver.

Charitable Remainder Unitrust

A charitable remainder unitrust is a trust with noncharitable beneficiaries, followed by charitable beneficiaries. The unitrust provides that the noncharitable beneficiaries receive an annual payment of the lesser of the trust's net income or a fixed percentage of the net fair market value of trust assets. The payments must continue for the life of the noncharitable beneficiary or for a term of years not to exceed 20 years, with the unitrust remainder going to charity upon the termination of the unitrust.

A gift of appreciated property, such as family business stock, to a unitrust is deductible for federal income tax purposes up to 30% of the owner's adjusted gross income in the year of the gift and for the next five years. The amount of the charitable income tax deduction is equal to the value of the future interest that will belong to charity.

Such a gift is deductible for federal transfer tax purposes without limitation. A unitrust pays *no federal income tax on the capital gain realized upon the sale* of the appreciated property by the unitrust. Income tax is paid by the noncharitable beneficiary only on distribution from the unitrust.

HYPOTHETICAL CASE OF JAMES AND SALLY FOUNDER: Each is 65 years old, with a combined estate worth $6.5 million. Of this total, $1 million is invested in publicly traded securities (with a low federal income tax basis) that provide the couple with a 1% annual return.

The couple's goal is to benefit their favorite charity while converting their securities into assets that will produce a higher annual return for their benefit. Furthermore, they want to accomplish this conversion without paying federal income taxes on the asset switch, thus leveraging the full investment power of their assets for themselves and ultimately for the charity of their choice.

The Founders create the unitrust, funding it with the $1 million in publicly traded securities. The unitrust, in turn, pays the couple 8% of the value of the trust's assets on an annual basis.

If this sounds appealing, it gets better. Although the Founders have converted their assets into a higher-yielding portfolio, they do not have to pay a tax on the capital gain reflected in the conversion of the assets given to the unitrust. What's more, the gift to the unitrust will generate an income tax deduction for the donors, based on the future value (or the remainder value) of the gift to the charity. At the Founders' age, this deduction is approximately $220,000.

The tax benefits skewed to the Founders are exceptional. Based on a 28% bracket, the federal income tax savings produced by the $220,000 deduction comes to about $61,000. This results from the federal income tax charitable deduction.

Making a good thing better, the $1 million gift to the unitrust translates into federal estate tax savings of $550,000 (based on the federal estate tax charitable deduction). Further, the chosen charity will receive all the assets in the unitrust when both Mr. and Mrs. Founder are deceased.

As with all financial transactions, there are drawbacks to charitable remainder trusts. Most important, you cede control of the assets to the trust once the gift is made. Before taking this approach, you must ask yourself if you are prepared to do this, relinquishing future appreciation as well as the opportunity to pass the assets to your heirs.

Life Insurance Trust

Perhaps the most effective way to provide liquidity to an estate and have enough funds to pay federal estate taxes is to purchase life insurance. Generally, life insurance proceeds are included in the gross estate of the deceased. However, these proceeds can be removed from the estate if the insurance is purchased inside an **irrevocable life insurance trust**.

A look at the mathematics of life insurance proves without a doubt why most people find it to be the best method of solving an estate tax problem. Suppose an individual has an estate tax liability of $500,000. If there is no insurance, nine months after death, her heirs must liquidate enough of the estate assets to pay the tax, resulting in a $500,000 shrinkage of their inheritance.

The estate holder could have spent a small amount of money for enough life insurance to settle the estate tax liability and pass the value of the full estate to the heirs.

Irrevocable life insurance trusts provide liquidity for the payment of estate taxes without creating greater estate tax liability and without using the unified credit. They can also be used to fund the grantor's obligations, such as alimony or child support, that continue after death.

These trusts are typically funded with annual gifts (covered by the gift tax exclusion of $10,000 per donor or $20,000 per couple), which are used to pay the insurance premiums. To qualify for the gift tax exclusion, a beneficiary must be permitted to withdraw assets given to the trust for a period of time following the gift. This is known as the **Crummey withdrawal power.** The gift tax exclusion also applies if the Crummey beneficiary does not exercise the withdrawal privilege and allows that privilege to lapse.

Advantages of Irrevocable Life Insurance Trusts

+ Life insurance proceeds are removed from the grantor's estate, providing the grantor is not the trustee.
+ Proceeds are available to provide liquidity to the grantor's estate for the purpose of paying taxes or purchasing assets (such as a family business) that the grantor would rather have out of the estate.
+ Distribution of trust assets can be coordinated with the overall estate plan.
+ Proceeds may be removed from the liability of the grantor's debts providing the grantor is not insolvent after making gifts to the trust or the gifts to the trust are not made with the intention of defrauding the grantor's present or future creditors.

Disadvantages of Irrevocable Life Insurance Trusts

− As the name implies, the trust is irrevocable and the grantor must relinquish complete control of the assets.
− The grantor cannot be the trustee for distribution purposes without inclusion in the grantor's estate.
− If the grantor wants the gifts to the trust to qualify for the annual gift tax exclusion, the beneficiary must have the authority to withdraw the gifts as they are made.
− If the grantor/insured dies within three years of the trust's receipt or acquisition of the life insurance policy, the proceeds may be included in the grantor's estate.

Don't Put It Off

The most important point to note about estate planning is that everyone needs to do it regardless of age or wealth. Too often this planning is put off until it is simply too late to make a significant impact. Each individual makes the conscious decision to pay estate tax or not, simply by taking the proper action to reduce this burden. Here are four key questions you should ask yourself:

1. Have you executed a will?
2. Is your will up-to-date?
3. Do you have significant assets to protect?
4. Have you planned how you will distribute your assets to your heirs?

If you have significant assets to protect, it is important that you take steps immediately to do so. The drafting of legal documents, such as a will or trust, should be done by a competent attorney.

Chapter 11

An Investor's Life Cycle

One ship drives east and another west, while the self-same
breezes blow; 'Tis the set of the sail and not the gale, that
bids them where to go.

Author Unknown

In this book, you have learned how a diversified portfolio of investments
can help you to achieve a higher standard of living and, ultimately, financial independence. You have also learned about establishing a college
fund for your children, wills, life insurance, estate planning, and other
areas of financial planning.

Now you may be asking, "At what age should I begin thinking about
each kind of investment?"

A Lifetime of Planning

Obviously, we want you to start thinking about your financial future right
now—no matter your current age. You're never too young to launch an
IRA, invest in your company's 401(k) plan, or begin an education fund
(even for children who have not yet been born!).

At the latest, a young person should begin serious financial planning
upon getting married and having a child. Life insurance, health insurance, disability insurance, and property and casualty insurance should
be acquired at this time. A college fund should be established, and a will
should be executed.

By middle age, your investment portfolio should be designed to raise
your standard of living and lay the groundwork for a financially independent retirement. You should have an emergency fund for personal or professional crises. If you have neglected to purchase life insurance or to set
up a college fund for a growing child, you should take these steps as soon
as possible. If you have fallen into debt over the years, you should begin
a systematic debt management plan immediately.

Senior citizens should focus on maximizing their yields in order to meet the living expenses of retirement—and to make the most of their golden years. They should also work to preserve their wealth for their heirs through estate planning.

Exhibit 11-1 should help you to prioritize your financial planning needs.

Financial Planning Priorities for Different Age Groups

Remember, the priorities listed in Exhibit 11-1 are simply guidelines. The earlier you launch yourself toward all of your financial goals, the sooner you will have peace of mind—and the more time the "magic" of compounding will have to work for you.

✳ Check off any questions on the Taxpayer Profile that you have not yet answered. If you are unsure how to respond, consult with a tax and financial professional.

Revisiting the 10 Principles

And now, let's revisit our 10 Principles of Successful Investing, with a few reminders of what you have learned.

1. *Self-discipline, not income level, determines your ability to save money.* Remember, if a family with an income of $50,000 a year saves $500 a month, it has the same opportunity for financial freedom as a family with an annual income of $500,000 that saves the same amount.

2. *If your "safe" investments don't outpace inflation, then your investments are not truly safe.* Because many people equate investing with losing money, they seek out investments that are guaranteed or insured. Banks often play to this by beating the drum of "safety" in their advertising, using phrases such as *insured against loss.* This leads investors to focus exclusively on "security" at the expense of growth.

Say the word *risk* to many people and their knee-jerk response is fear. Instead of recognizing that there are levels of risk associated with levels of reward, they view risk as an all-or-nothing proposition. With this mind-set, either you invest and accept the risk of losing your money or you put your money in "safe" instruments and eliminate risk.

Exhibit 11-1. Financial planning priorities for different age groups.

Young (Ages 20-40)

1.   Execute a Will(s)

2.   Health Insurance

3.   Disability Insurance

4.   Property and Casualty

*Middle Age
(Ages 40-60)*

5.   Life Insurance

6.   Emergency Fund

7.   Debt Management

8.   College Funding

9.   Financial Independence

10.   Higher Standard of Living

*Senior Citizen
(Ages 60+)*

11.   Yield Maximization

12.   Estate Planning

13.   Special Wants

But this simplistic and erroneous view of risk fails to account for the fact that "safe" instruments can carry a higher level of risk because of the lower yields generally associated with them and because of their exposure to inflation. In most cases, these are the real risks you should be focusing on.

3. *Don't try to "time" the stock market to succeed as a stock market investor; those who try it usually fail.* There will always be bull and bear market cycles, as well as major upheavals that dramatically affect market prices temporarily. But history indicates that the market has always recovered and that patience, rather than timing, prevails.

Furthermore, if you are waiting for the "perfect" time to invest, chances are you will never invest at all—and never begin accumulating wealth. That's because there are always debts to pay and luxuries to buy; if you wait until all of these temptations and obligations are out of the way, you will find yourself far, far removed from the goal of achieving financial independence. The fact is, *now* is the time to invest, because the sooner you get started, the more you will accumulate.

4. *Your investments should be part of an overall strategy designed to achieve your specific financial objectives.* Most people think that investing is a series of reactions to day-to-day events. Nothing could be further from the truth. The key point is that investing should be a deliberate process, with set goals, where success is measured in years, not days or weeks.

College funds, retirement funds, and other investment programs all require specific strategies. Working together, they form a coherent, efficient financial plan.

5. *Substantial growth of assets over the long term requires some equity investments, which can be volatile. The percentage of equities in your portfolio should be compatible with your tolerance for risk.* We all drive at different speeds. If you were a passenger in a race car driven by Mario Andretti, you might be tempted to panic and leap from the vehicle (obviously, a dangerous decision). It is similarly risky to choose an investment whose fluctuations will tempt you to sell it at the wrong time.

6. *The most efficient portfolios are properly diversified, both within and among the basic asset categories. Diversification* is another way of saying, "Don't put your eggs in one basket." It is the key to creating a portfolio that matches your goals and risk tolerance.

A mutual fund, you have learned, offers built-in diversification by spreading your investments within and/or among the major asset categories. Purchasing additional mutual funds can help you achieve the ideal mix of investments, customized to satisfy your risk tolerance, time frame, and investment objectives.

7. *The most successful investors are patient, long-term investors.* Investing for the long term is the only way to take full advantage of the twin miracles of time and compounding. Sometimes referred to as the eighth wonder of the world, time and compounding are the hidden power that makes a well-conceived investment plan work.

The tragedy is that many investors—those who fail to understand this concept—lose their patience and move out of investments before time and compounding have had the chance to work.

8. *Investing should be as systematic as paying a monthly bill.* Pay yourself first. By treating your investment plan as a monthly bill—taking the first $50, $100, or $500 from your paycheck and making sure you invest it each month—you instill investment discipline. This type of systematic investing, known as dollar cost averaging, also permits you to capitalize on market cycles and come out a winner in the end.

9. *You should take a holistic approach to your financial life, recognizing that tax strategies, insurance needs, and investment goals are interrelated.* Quite simply, this has been the guiding principle of this book.

10. *You should find a knowledgeable tax and financial advisor you can trust.* We believe that for most Americans, there is no better advisor than a tax professional who offers financial planning services. Whoever you choose, make sure the person is not transaction-oriented, and that he or she has your best interests at heart.

The Next Step

We have explored the major options and strategies for accumulating wealth and achieving financial freedom. We've warned you of the mistakes most commonly made by investors and would-be investors. And we have asked you to complete the Taxpayer Profile in Appendix A to draw a sketch of your financial situation.

Now, we urge you to take the next logical step. Take your completed Taxpayer Profile, along with last year's 1040 form, and visit your tax professional to develop a personal financial plan. Then put that plan into action.

If your tax professional is not licensed to provide you with the financial products you need, you may call 1-800-4-WEALTH, and our associates at H. D. Vest Financial Services will help you locate a qualified professional near you. If your current accountant is a trusted advisor but does not currently offer the products and services you need, you should urge your advisor to call the 800 number so that he or she may join the growing nationwide network of H. D. Vest representatives.

It was Ralph Waldo Emerson who said, "Fear is born of ignorance." Because most people fail to educate themselves about investing, they resort to investing by fear. With knowledge—and sound professional advice—you can build the confidence to embark on the journey to financial freedom. Don't delay; the sooner you begin, the more likely you will reach your destination.

Appendix A

Taxpayer Profile

TAXPAYER PROFILE

Name: _____ **Spouse Name:** _____

Tax Return Reviewed - For the year ended_____

Form 1040 - Exemptions

	You	**Spouse**
	Needs Review (Y or N)	

Spouse: Working (Y or N)

	You	Spouse
Will	_____	_____
Life Ins.	_____	_____
Disability	_____	_____
Health	_____	_____
Property & Casualty	_____	_____

Dependents: Children's Names	SS# (Y or N)	Years Until College	Start Education Fund (Y or N)	Dollars Needed	Years in College
_____	_____	_____	_____	_____	_____
_____	_____	_____	_____	_____	_____
_____	_____	_____	_____	_____	_____
_____	_____	_____	_____	_____	_____

To Do: _____Develop/review of Will
_____Insurance review
_____Life
_____Disability
_____Health
_____Property & Casualty
_____Long-term Care
_____Establish educational fund(s)
_____Prepare form SS-5 for dependent Social Security number
_____Invest up to $1,200 in tax-exempt or tax-deferred
investments for children who are younger than 14
and whose parents are in a high tax bracket

Form 1040 - Line 7
Wages

Are you or is your spouse an executive, a highly paid   θ   Yes   θ   No
employee or an owner or partner in a business?

To Do: _____Establish or contribute to company
contribution plans
_____SEP
_____Keogh
_____Corporate
_____Defined Benefit

_____Establish or contribute to employee
salary reduction plans
    _____SAR-SEP
    _____401(k)
_____Establish or contribute to nonqualified
deferred compensation plans
    _____Salary Continuation Plan
    _____Executive Bonus Plan
_____Establish or contribute to group insurance plans
    _____Health
    _____Life
    _____Disability
_____Establish or contribute to key person
insurance plans
    _____Life
    _____Disability

Are you or is your spouse an employee of   θ Yes   θ No
a tax-exempt organization?

To Do: _____Contribute to plan of 403(b) or 501(c)(3) organizations -
employees of public schools, hospitals, or
charitable organizations

Are you or is your spouse an employee of a state   θ Yes   θ No
or local government?

To Do: _____Contribute to 457 plan - state and local government
employees

Form 1040 - Lines 8a and 9

Schedule B -   **Taxable Interest** $_____
    Taxable Dividends $_____

Do you have an existing investment portfolio?   θ Yes   θ No

To Do: _____Analyze portfolio and review financial objectives
_____Change broker/dealer
_____Use asset allocation model

Do you have individual stocks and bonds?   θ Yes   θ No

To Do: _____Reinvest into diversified portfolio
_____Use asset allocation model

Do you have CDs?   θ Yes   θ No

To Do: _____Rollover to higher yielding investments
_____Reinvest into diversified portfolio
_____Use asset allocation model
_____Tax-deferred annuity or tax-exempt investment

Are you in a high tax bracket? Tax Bracket _____%   θ Yes   θ No

To Do: _____Review tax-exempt investments such as municipal bonds
_____Review tax-deferred investments such as annuities
_____Review tax credits or tax-sheltered investments such
as partnerships

No Investments?   θ Yes   θ No

To Do: _____Start monthly savings plan
_____Establish emergency fund
_____Reduce debt
_____Other

Form 1040 - Line 8b

Tax-exempt Interest Income $_____

Is yield competitive considering tax bracket?   θ   Yes   θ   No

If no, consider taxable investments or tax swaps to a higher
yielding security

Are you properly diversified?   θ   Yes   θ   No

If no, consider selling individual bonds and buy UITs or
mutual funds

Are you currently using income?   θ   Yes   θ   No

If no, consider annuities

Form 1040 - Lines 12, 18 and 19

Schedule C - Business Income or Loss
Schedule E - Partnerships - Working Partner
Schedule F - Farm Income or Loss

Are you or is your spouse self-employed or a working partner?   θ   Yes   θ   No

To Do: _____Establish qualified retirement plan
                      _____SEP
                      _____Keogh
                      _____401(k)
                      _____SAR/SEP
                _____Group Insurance Plan
                _____Key Person Insurance Plan
                _____Disability Income Plan

Form 1040 - Line 13

Schedule D - Capital Gain or Loss

Do you have capital gains that are not being   θ   Yes   θ   No
offset by capital losses?

To Do: _____Consider bond, stock, mutual fund or
                      UIT tax swaps to create capital losses

Do you have capital assets?   θ   Yes   θ   No

To Do: _____Review assets
                _____Identify investment alternatives
                _____Generate capital losses to offset gains/
                      ordinary income

Do you have unrealized capital losses?   θ   Yes   θ   No

To Do: _____Generating capital gains through
                      sale of specific assets

Form 1040 - Line 18

Schedule E - Rents, Royalties, Partnerships, Estates and Trusts

Do you have existing passive losses?   θ   Yes   θ   No

To Do: _____Consider passive income generator

Do you have existing passive income?   θ   Yes   θ   No

To Do: _____Consider passive activity loss generator

Are you interested in nonpassive investments?   θ   Yes   θ   No

To Do: _____Review working interest oil and
                      gas joint venture

Do you have existing income from estate or trust?   θ   Yes   θ   No

To Do: _____Review estate/trust assets for return and
                      suitability

Are you in a high tax bracket?   θ   Yes   θ   No

To Do: _____Consider tax-sheltered partnerships

_____Consider tax-credit partnerships

Do you have existing income from rents or royalties?   θ   Yes   θ   No

To Do: _____Determine sources of income

_____Review for suitability, return and liquidity

Form 1040 - Line 21

Social Security Benefits

Do you have to pay taxes on your   θ   Yes   θ   No
Social Security benefits?

To Do: _____Consider partnership investments

_____Consider tax-deferred annuities or
single premium whole life

Form 1040 - Lines 16a, 17a and 24

**Pensions, IRA Distributions, Annuities and Current IRA
Deduction**

Did you make a current year IRA contribution?   θ   Yes   θ   No

To Do: _____Determine deductibility and
make contribution

Did you receive rollovers/lump-sum distributions?   θ   Yes   θ   No

To Do: _____Complete transfer or rollover

_____Use asset allocation model

Do you have existing IRAs?   θ   Yes   θ   No

To Do: _____Consolidate

_____Use asset allocation model

Have you contributed to next year's IRA?   θ   Yes   θ   No

To Do: _____Early funding in monthly
installments

Form 1040 - Line 26

Self-employed Health Insurance Deduction

Are you self-employed, and do you have health   θ   Yes   θ   No
insurance?

To Do: _____Establish health insurance program

Form 1040 - Line 27

Keogh Retirement Plan and Self-employed SEP Deduction

Do you have an existing Keogh?   θ   Yes   θ   No

To Do: _____Make current year contribution

_____Transfer assets

_____Analyze assets and investment alternatives

Do you have an existing SEP?   θ   Yes   θ   No

To Do: _____Make current year contribution

_____Transfer assets

_____Analyze assets and investment alternatives

Form 1040 - Line 34

Itemized Deductions

Do you pay health/medical insurance premiums?   θ   Yes   θ   No

To Do: _____Review/obtain medical
insurance

Do you have nondeductible interest expense?   θ   Yes   θ   No

To Do: _____Pay off debt
          _____Consider equity loan

Do you have nondeductible investment interest expense?   θ   Yes   θ   No

To Do: _____Pay off debt/increase investment income

Have you made charitable contributions?   θ   Yes   θ   No

To Do: _____Consider Charitable Remainder Trust
          _____Consider Irrevocable Life Insurance Trust

Form 1040 - Lines 10 and 62

**State and Local Income
Tax Refunds**   \$_____

Federal Income Tax Refund   \$_____

Will you receive a refund?   θ   Yes   θ   No

To Do: _____Review investment alternatives
          _____Reduce withholding
          _____Start monthly savings plan
          _____Fund IRA

Appendix B

H. D. Vest Retirement Plan Guide

(Caution: New Rules and Interpretations are constantly being made that may affect the plans listed below. This guide is intended as general information only. When you implement a plan, please call H.D. Vest if you need assistance or to check for any changes to the rules listed below.)

CAPABILITIES/ RESTRICTIONS	MONEY PURCHASE (*Defined Contribution*)	PROFIT SHARING (*Defined Contribution*)	SEP-IRA (*Simplified Employee Pension*)	SAR-SEP (*Salary Reduction SEP*)	KEOGH	401(k) PROFIT SHARING (*Defined Contribution*)	IRA	403(B) TAX-SHELTERED ANNUITIES	PENSION PLAN (*Defined Benefit*)	457 PLANS
Definition Of	Plan has a contribution formula in which the employer promises to contribute a definite amount each year as a % of compensation or salary on behalf of each participant. All contributions plus earnings are allocated to individual accounts which determine the individual's benefit at retirement.	The formula for determining the amount of the employer's contribution is fully discretionary. It is based on a % of compensation or salary on behalf of each participant. All contributions plus earnings are allocated to individual accounts which determine the individual's benefit at retirement.	A simplified employee pension is a plan through which employer contributions are made to IRA accounts established and maintained by eligible employees. These tax deductible contributions must be allocated by the employer on a non-discriminatory basis.	A salary reduction SEP allows for employee contributions through salary deferrals. This feature is available only to employers with 25 or fewer eligible employees through the preceding year. At least half of all eligible employees must participate each year.	A Keogh is a plan designed for sole proprietorships and partnerships. They allow smaller businesses to enjoy the advantages of a qualified plan. A Keogh plan consists of either a money purchase or profit-sharing plan, or both.	Plan permits a deferred arrangement as part of an employer's profit-sharing or stock bonus plan. The arrangement may be in the form of salary reduction between the employer and employee under which a contribution will be made only if the employee elects to reduce his compensation or forego a salary increase. Special nondiscriminatory tests apply. 125% Actual Deferral Percentage (ADP) or 200% ADP plus the excess cannot exceed 2%.	Individual retirement savings arrangements to which contributions are made by an individual based on compensation. The deductibility of the IRA contribution is dependent upon the individual's income and participation in qualified retirement plans.	Tax-sheltered retirement program established by 501(C)(3) organizations and public schools for their employees. Plan may be funded on a nondiscriminatory basis through salary reduction or deferral of salary increase and may only invest in annuities or mutual funds.	Plan is established so that the amount of the employee's retirement income is fixed defining the benefit in advance by the plan's benefit formula. The employer's contribution must be determined actuarially and be sufficient to enable the fund to meet its liabilities as they come due in future years.	Tax-sheltered retirement program established by federal, municipal and county government agencies.
Obligation To Contribution	Employer must meet minimum funding requirement.	Contributions are at the discretion of the employer and are not dependent on profits.	Employer makes voluntary contributions and can change each year or discontinue.	Nondiscrimination tests must be met. 125% Actual Deferral Percentages (ADP) rule for key employees vs. nonhighly compensated.	Profit sharing - Optional; Money Purchase - Mandatory.	Contributions can come from salary that employees have chosen to defer, employer contributions, or both.	Individual makes voluntary contributions.	Contributions can come from salary that employees have chosen to defer, employer contributions or both.	Employer must meet minimum funding requirements, dictated by the benefit formula.	No employer contribution can be made. Plan is funded solely by salary deferral.

CAPABILITIES/ RESTRICTIONS	MONEY PURCHASE (Defined Contribution)	PROFIT SHARING (Defined Contribution)	SEP-IRA (Simplified Employee Pension)	SAR-SEP (Salary Reduction SEP)	KEOGH	401(k) PROFIT SHARING (Defined Contribution)	IRA	403(B) TAX-SHELTERED ANNUITIES	PENSION PLAN (Defined Benefit)	457 PLANS
Maximum Deductible Contribution	25% of participant's compensation or $30,000, whichever is less.	Employer deduction cannot exceed 15% of aggregate participant's compensation. Allocation to each participant cannot exceed 15% of compensation or $30,000, whichever is less.	Employer deduction cannot exceed 15% of aggregate participant's compensation. Allocation to each participant cannot exceed 15% of compensation or $30,000, whichever is less.	Salary reduction amount cannot exceed 15% of participant's compensation or $8,994.	20% of earned income or $30,000, whichever is less. If profit sharing only is chosen, a maximum of 13.043% of earned income can be contributed. Net schedule C less 1/2 of SE tax paid times contribution percentage. (20% or 13.043% for applicable plan.)	Employer contributions together with salary reduction cannot exceed lesser of 25% of compensation or $30,000. Employer deduction limits are the same as for profit-sharing plans. Salary reduction amount cannot exceed $8,994.	If not active participant in qualified plan: Lesser of: a) 100% of compensation, or b) $2,000 ($2,250 for spousal IRA) If individual or spouse participates in qualified plan, contribution is reduced and then eliminated for adjusted gross income between $40,000 and $50,000 (married) and $25,000 and $35,000 (single).	The maximum deferral is $9,500 annually (reduced by elective 401(k) and SAR-SEP contributions).	Amount needed to fund monthly benefit at normal retirement age. Annual benefit from the plan may not exceed $115,641 with retirement at age 65.	Salary reduction amount cannot exceed 33 1/3% of includible compensation or $7,500 whichever is less (not indexed for inflation). 403(b) contributions included in $7,500 calculation. Catch-up - Maximum $15,000 available last 3 years before retirement.
Prospects	Company with stable yearly profits (no problem contributing in good or bad years), low employee turnover.	Best suited for relatively new company or a cyclical company with high turnover. Usually better than money purchase if desired contribution rate does not exceed 15% of payroll.	Business owner who wants simplicity. Ideally suited for company with more volatile profits and low employee turnover. Business owners tired of filing requirements and amendments.	Employer with fewer than 25 employees at any time during the past year seeking the retirement plan funded by employee contributions with minimal filings and paperwork.	For clients who want 25% of earned income as a contribution and do not want immediate vesting.	Best suited for employer who wants to minimize employer contributions. Usually suited for larger companies because of cost of administering the plan and to encourage employee savings.	Individuals with earned income. Rollovers from qualified plans and transfers from other IRAs.	Public schools or nonprofit organizations such as charitable religious groups, or hospitals.	Suited for established companies with consistent profits. Benefits companies with key employees over age 45.	Municipals and cities including fire departments, municipal utility districts and civil services.
Entity or Person Who Can Establish Plan	Corporation, Partnership, Self-Employed - See Keogh, S Corporations.	Corporation, Partnership, Self-Employed - See Keogh, S Corporations.	Corporation, Partnership, Self-Employed - See Keogh, S Corporations.	Corporation, Partnership, Self-Employed, S Corporations.	Sole Proprietorships, Partnerships.	Corporation, Partnership, Self-Employed, S Corporations.	Anyone with earned income.	Public Schools and Tax Exempt 501(C)(3) Organizations.	Corporation, Partnership, Self-Employed, S Corporations.	Federal, municipal and county government agency.
Eligibility	Possible exclusions: under age 21, employees who have worked less than 1,000 hours per year of service, less than 2 years of service. If more than 1 year is chosen, plan is subject to 100% immediate vesting.	Possible exclusions: under age 21, employees who have worked less than 1,000 hours per year of service, less than 2 years of service. If more than 1 year is chosen, plan is subject to 100% immediate vesting.	Includes all employees over age 21 who have worked for employer for any part of 3 of last 5 calendar years. May exclude employees earning less than $385 per year and union employees covered by a collective bargaining agreement.	Generally, employee participation is voluntary. At least 50% of eligible employees must participate.	Possible exclusions: under age 21, employees who have worked less than 1,000 hours per year of service, less than 2 years of service.	If more than 1 year is chosen, plan is subject to 100% immediate vesting.	Possible exclusions: under age 21, employees who have worked less than 1,000 hours per year of service, less than 1 year of service.	All persons with earned income who are under age 70 1/2.	Employees of public schools or 501(C)(3) organizations.	All employees of government organizations.

CAPABILITIES/ RESTRICTIONS	MONEY PURCHASE (*Defined Contribution*)	PROFIT SHARING (*Defined Contribution*)	SEP-IRA (*Simplified Employee Pension*)	SAR-SEP (*Salary Reduction SEP*)	KEOGH	401(k) PROFIT SHARING (*Defined Contribution*)	IRA	403(B) TAX-SHELTERED ANNUITIES	PENSION PLAN (*Defined Benefit*)	457 PLANS
Establishment/ Contribution Deadline	Must be established by tax year-end and contributions made by tax return due date, including extensions.	Must be established by tax year-end and contributions made by tax return due date, including extensions.	Must be established and contribution must be made by tax return due date, including extensions.	Must be established by year-end and contributions are deductible for the taxable year with or within which the calendar year ends.	Must be established by tax year-end and funding by tax return due date, including extensions.	Must be established by tax year-end and contributions made by tax year-end.	Must be established and contribution made by April 15th.	1. One salary reduction agreement per employee per calendar year. 2. Contribution based on a calendar year.	Must be established by tax year-end and contributions made by tax return due date, including extensions. Quarterly contributions required beginning in 1989.	1. Salary reduction agreement signed and contributions made on per paycheck basis. 2. All contributions made by year end.
Can Be Integrated with Social Security	Yes	Yes	Yes	No	Yes	Yes, if employer is making contributions. No, if 100% employee funded.	No	Yes, if employer is making contributions. No, if 100% employee funded.	Yes	No
Vesting Requirements	Must meet ERISA minimum requirements or TEFRA minimum requirements. If top-heavy, use 3-year cliff, or 6-year graded vesting.	Must meet ERISA minimum requirements or TEFRA minimum requirements. If top-heavy, use 3-year cliff, or 6-year graded vesting.	Immediate 100% vesting.	Immediate 100% vesting.	Must meet ERISA minimum requirements or TEFRA minimum requirements. If top-heavy, use 3-year cliff, or 6-year graded vesting.	On employee elective deferrals, immediate 100%. Employer contributions, ERISA minimum requirements or TEFRA minimum requirements if top-heavy.	Immediate 100% vesting.	Immediate 100% vesting of employee contributions.	Must meet ERISA minimum requirements or TEFRA minimum requirements. If top-heavy, use 3-year cliff, or 6-year graded vesting.	N/A. Salary deferrals are 100% vested.
Minimum Contribution/ Benefit for Top-heavy Plans	Up to 3% of compensation to all nonkey employee participants or same % of compensation applicable to highly compensated employee.	Up to 3% of compensation to all nonkey employee participants or same % of compensation applicable to highly compensated employee.	Contribution made must be the same % of each employee's total compensation.	Up to 3% of compensation to all nonkey employee participants or same % of compensation applicable to highly compensated employee.	Up to 3% of compensation to all nonkey employee participants or same % of compensation applicable to highly compensated employee.	Up to 3% of compensation to all nonkey employee participants or same % of compensation applicable to highly compensated employee.	Not applicable.	Must be available to all eligible employees; may exclude people in 457 or qualified CODAs.	Minimum benefit of lesser of 2% of compensation times years of service or 20% of average compensation for non-key employee participants.	All employees are eligible to participate.
Distributions/ Withdrawals Prior to Age 59 1/2 Unless Termination Disability or Death Occurs	10% penalty applies to withdrawals before age 59 1/2. The 10% penalty is replaced by a 15% excise tax on distributions over $150,000 per calendar year.	10% penalty applies to withdrawals before age 59 1/2. The 10% penalty is replaced by a 15% excise tax on distributions over $150,000 per calendar year.	10% penalty applies to withdrawals before age 59 1/2. The 10% penalty is replaced by a 15% excise tax on distributions over $150,000 per calendar year.	10% penalty applies to withdrawals before age 59 1/2. The 10% penalty is replaced by a 15% excise tax on distributions over $150,000 per calendar year.	10% penalty applies to withdrawals before age 59 1/2. The 10% penalty is replaced by a 15% excise tax on distributions over $150,000 per calendar year.	10% penalty applies to withdrawals before age 59 1/2. The 10% penalty is replaced by a 15% excise tax on distributions over $150,000 per calendar year.	10% penalty applies to withdrawals before age 59 1/2. The 10% penalty is replaced by a 15% excise tax on distributions over $150,000 per calendar year.	10% penalty applies to withdrawals before age 59 1/2. The 10% penalty is replaced by a 15% excise tax on distributions over $150,000 per calendar year.	10% penalty applies to withdrawals before age 59 1/2. The 10% penalty is replaced by a 15% excise tax on distributions over $150,000 per calendar year.	Distributions not eligible for rollover. Must pay tax on any distributions. Participant may elect to keep account until retirement or until income is needed. Not a qualified plan- 10% withdrawal penalty does not apply.

Capabilities/ Restrictions	Money Purchase (Defined Contribution)	Profit Sharing (Defined Contribution)	SEP-IRA (Simplified Employee Pension)	SAR-SEP (Salary Reduction SEP)	Keogh	401(k) Profit Sharing (Defined Contribution)	IRA	403(B) Tax-Sheltered Annuities	Pension Plan (Defined Benefit)	457 Plans
Loans	Loan privileges must be stated in plan document and repaid within a 5-year period (except when the loan is for purchasing a principal residence) and level amortization payments must be made quarterly. The **outstanding** loan balance cannot exceed the lesser of $50,000 or 50% of the participant's vested accrued benefit. A plan's limit can never be less than $10,000.	Loan privileges must be stated in plan document and repaid within a 5-year period (except when the loan is for purchasing a principal residence) and level amortization payments must be made quarterly. The **outstanding** loan balance cannot exceed the lesser of $50,000 or 50% of the participant's vested accrued benefit. A plan's limit can never be less than $10,000.	Not Allowed.	Not Allowed.	Not allowed for owner employees unless special exemption from Department of Labor. Allowed for common law employees with restrictions same as profit-sharing plan.	Loans must be repaid within a 5-year period (except when the loan is for purchasing a principal residence) and level amortization payments must be made quarterly. The **outstanding** loan balance cannot exceed the lesser of $50,000 or 50% of the participant's vested accrued benefit. A plan's limit can never be less than $10,000.	Not Allowed.	Loans must be repaid within a 5-year period (except when the loan is for purchasing a principal residence) and level amortization payments must be made quarterly. The **outstanding** loan balance cannot exceed the lesser of $50,000 or 50% of the participant's vested accrued benefit. A plan's limit can never be less than $10,000.	Loans must be repaid within a 5-year period (except when the loan is for purchasing a principal residence) and level amortization payments must be made quarterly. The **outstanding** loan balance cannot exceed the lesser of $50,000 or 50% of the participant's vested accrued benefit. A plan's limit can never be less than $10,000.	Not Allowed.
What Happens When the Employee Leaves? (Forfeiture)	Forfeited funds may be reallocated among remaining participants, or may be used to reduce employer contributions.	Forfeited funds may be reallocated among remaining participants, or may be used to reduce employer contributions.	Unaffected by terminations.	Unaffected by terminations.	Forfeited funds may be reallocated among remaining participants, or may be used to reduce employer contributions.	Forfeited funds may be reallocated among remaining participants, or may be used to reduce employer contributions. Employee deferrals are 100% vested.	Unaffected by terminations.	Unaffected by terminations.	Forfeited funds are used to reduce subsequent contributions.	Account can remain with employer and is tax deferred. Account can be transferred to a new 457 plan. No rollover option.
Reporting and Disclosure	Full ERISA requirements. IRS Forms 5500, 5500-C, 5500-EZ or 5500-R annually.	Full ERISA requirements. IRS Forms 5500, 5500-C, 5500-EZ or 5500-R annually.	Minimal. Employer fills out IRS Form 5305-SEP and gives copy to plan participants.	Minimal. Employer fills out IRS Form 5305A-SEP and gives copies to plan participants.	Full ERISA requirements. IRS Forms 5500, 5500-C, 5500-EZ or 5500-R annually.	Full ERISA requirements. IRS Forms 5500, 5500-C or 5500-R annually.	Deductible contributions shown on Form 1040, individual return. File IRS Form 8606 for nondeductible contributions.	May require full ERISA requirements. IRS Forms 5500, 5500-C or 5500-R annually if employer is contributing.	Full ERISA requirements. IRS Forms 5500, 5500-C or 5500-R annually.	No 5500s to be filed.

Index